Foucault and Derrida
THE OTHER SIDE OF REASON

Foucault and Derrida

THE OTHER SIDE OF REASON

Roy Boyne

London and New York

First published 1990
by Unwin Hyman Ltd

Reprinted 1994 and 1996
by Routledge
11 New Fetter Lane, London EC4P 4EE
29 West 35th Street, New York, NY 10001

Printed and bound in Great Britain by
Redwood Books, Trowbridge

British Library Cataloguing in Publication Data
A catalogue reference for this book is available from the British Library.

Library of Congress Cataloguing in Publication Data
A catalogue reference for this book is available from the Library of Congress.

ISBN 0–415–11916–2

Contents

List of plates   viii

Acknowledgements   ix

Introduction   1

1   *Foucault on Madness*   5

    The Political Economy of Madness   5
    Madness in Art and Literature   15
    Madness and Science   27
    Notes and References   34

2   *The Cartesian Exclusion*   36

    Foucault and Descartes   43
    Notes and References   50

3   *Derrida and Foucault*   53

    The Critique   55
    Foucault's Replies   71
    The Question of Transgression   80
    Notes and References   87

4   *The Text and the Body*   90

    Deconstruction   90
    Discipline and Punish   109
    Notes and References   119

5   *Post-Hierarchical Politics*   123

    Derrida, Foucault and Marxism   125
    Feminism and Difference   135
    Race and Difference   152
    Notes and References   160

Conclusion: Difference and the Other   166

Bibliography   171

Index   177

List of plates

1   *The Cure of Madness* by Hieronymus Bosch (Prado, Madrid)

2   *The Ship of Fools* by Hieronymus Bosch (The Louvre, Paris)

3   *The Temptation of St Anthony* (detail) by Hieronymus Bosch (Museu Nacional de Arte Antiga, Lisbon)

4   *The Triumph of Death* by Peter Brueghel (Prado, Madrid)

5   *Dulle Griet* by Peter Brueghel (Musee Mayer van den Bergh, Antwerp)

6   *Horsemen of the Apocalypse* by Albrecht Durer (British Museum, London)

7   *Caprichos No. 43* by Goya (British Museum, London)

8   *The Witches' Sabbath* by Goya (Prado, Madrid)

Acknowledgements

I would like to thank Zygmunt Bauman and Janet Wolff, who both supported this work from the beginning. Rosalind Boyne gave much support in its early stages. The SSRC, as it was then, provided funding for a period of study in France. My colleagues at Newcastle Polytechnic covered teaching for me, so that I could concentrate on the book at a crucial stage. Library staff at the Polytechnic, especially Philip Judd, were unfailingly helpful. John O'Neill, Bryan Turner, Scott Lash, Richard Kilminster and Richard Roberts all read parts of the manuscript and offered helpful support and criticism. Most of all, however, I am grateful to Nicky Turnbull. She has caused me to question some of my deepest prejudices. I have learnt much from her, and continue to do so.

Introduction

In many ways this book is a kind of detective story. It tries to find something out about the kind of society which is taking shape in these last years of the century. No doubt the empirical sociologist will be aghast to find that, instead of an examination of structural social change in, for example, Europe and North America, the solid core of the investigation concerns the nature of madness, the birth of the prison, problems of textual interpretation, the nature of the self in ancient Greece, and forms of theorizing current within socialist, feminist and anti-racialist movements. But forensic procedures are not always obvious, and in this case they lead to certain hypotheses about our present and future which perhaps could not have been easily arrived at in any other way.

The story begins with an academic debate. In 1961 a young French philosopher named Michel Foucault published a lengthy treatise on the history of madness. This original and controversial work has since been criticized for its inaccuracies, its parochialism, its neglect of long tracts of historical time, its romanticism and the tortuousness of its gnomic pronouncements. But only one critical response really hit the mark. It came two years after the book's initial publication, in the form of a spoken presentation given by Jacques Derrida – a philosopher of literature who was to become famous as the founder of deconstruction, which is a rigorous and contentious kind of textual criticism.

Superficially the debate, at times acrimonious, between Foucault and Derrida was not about madness at all, but about the patriarch of Western philosophy, René Descartes. However, to an extent perhaps underappreciated by the participants themselves, the real object of their dispute was the nature of Western thought: is it possible to imagine a complete restructuring of the way we think?

Both of these philosophers had powerful reasons, as we shall see, for holding to their respective positions. But, away from the heat and light of their direct confrontation, and long after the discussion appeared to be over, the two protagonists proceeded along paths which would eventually cross. The point at which they finally do so is the common ground of power and ethics.

As far as power is concerned, it might be thought that such a development is hardly surprising. After all, the concept of power is central to most of the frameworks which are applied, in the pursuit of rigorous understanding, to social phenomena. So even though they developed interests in different things after their public disagreement, the mere fact that they both came to appreciate the importance of power for the things they studied should not of itself be of any particular importance. In the normal course of events that would be so. But in this case, the understanding of power in Derrida's work is only implicit, while, in Foucault's work, it is quite explicit. Nothing arises out of this until two things are realized: first, that Foucault's understanding of power seeks to break with all the traditional forms of understanding social relations; and second, that the concept of power that is only implicit in Derrida's work is made explicit by Foucault, for whom in doing so hardly a thought of Derrida crosses his mind.

When we consider the question of ethics, and let us be quite specific, of Kantian ethics, what seems further remarkable is that both Foucault and Derrida arrive, at the end of their trajectories, at an affirmation of one law above all others. That law is effectively the categorical imperative that human beings should never be treated as means alone, that the foundation of right behaviour is to be sought in the idea of the universalizability of the principles according to which one acts. That such ideas should appear to be their joint destination is especially noteworthy given not only their animosity to one another, but also their shared scepticism and hostility to the main lines of Western philosophy. It is as if both thinkers were separately engaged, from their different points of view, in the same test of reason, at the end of which they found certain elements therein that could not be denied.

We have, then, a remarkable turn around. Two philosophical opponents leave their field of combat in a state of fundamental disagreement. They develop their work in different directions yet nevertheless meet up again in an unrecognized partnership of theoretical understanding.

This book seeks to chart the unconscious history of this partnership. The first chapter, while not aspiring to provide an exhaustive account of Foucault's first major work, will introduce his history of madness. In the second chapter, we will examine the idea that Descartes' thought is entirely complicit with the exclusion of madness from the developing civilization of the West. Derrida enters the scene in Chapter 3, which provides an extended account of his philosophical dispute with Foucault. Chapter 4 takes us beyond their direct confrontation and shows, through a comparison of Foucault's work on the history of the prison and some of the main texts of deconstruction, how their underlying assumptions began to converge. The fifth and final chapter witnesses their arrival at the intersection of politics and ethics.

The circle is now complete. Foucault and Derrida both wrote in such a way that what they said could easily be taken as a challenge to, even a rejection of, the apparently self-satisfied ideals of liberalism, enlightenment and universal reason. Foucault, at the end of his life, however, effectively asks us to consider the contemporary significance of classical Greek ethics. His final request was that we should learn from the past how better to cope with the dilemmas of the present. From this perspective, it is hard, in the final analysis, to see him as an enemy of reason. Derrida, on the other hand, began by opposing Foucault with the classical philosophical tradition begun in ancient Greece. He did this not so as to celebrate reason, but rather so that the very difficult task of changing it might stand a better chance of success. For all his determination to deconstruct Western metaphysics, however, we find him at the end of his odyssey writing polemics against apartheid and fretful discourses about racism in the work and lives of Paul de Man and Martin Heidegger. This is not the work of a thoroughgoing relativist or even of a thoroughly postmodern pluralist.

It has to be admitted that thus far this appears to be a local issue, nothing more than one of those interesting episodes in the somewhat arcane reaches of contemporary philosophy. The argument of this book is that it is considerably more than this. This new intersection of realism with regard to power, from one direction, and idealist ethics, from another, has other origins. It will be found, often in a less articulated form, in writings emanating from what have been called the new social movements. It will also be found in new appraisals of bureaucracy, exemplified by such ideas as quality circles and anti-hierarchical organization. In short, a new view of social power, simultaneously anti-Utopian and non-fatalistic, is slowly taking shape in both the world of theory and the world of practice. Within this emerging vision, the final affirmation of ethics is crucial. For it tells us to beware of the mindless social violence which can be perpetrated by those representatives of the new pragmatic social order who do not recognize the immanent condition of humanity.

The history of civilization has been marked by struggles between the old and the new, and the phenomenon of resistance appears to be something approaching a universal. There are always interests which will be damaged by change, and which will therefore fight against it. In their debate, Foucault and Derrida misunderstood each other, each thinking the other to represent such interests. For Foucault, Derrida was a defender of the one form of understanding that would always remain the same, that would always produce holy wars in the name of truth, and sanctified divisions between the experts and the ignorant; for Derrida, Foucault's subtle defence of the established order was the false promise of Utopia, an image which if pursued would always lead to disillusionment and the acceptance that nothing can ever change the way that the world is.

But out of their confrontation, marginal though it might have been, there arises the thought, whispered elsewhere in different languages and in different ways, that the age of hierarchy is drawing to a close. The guiding spirit of their work tells us that desirable though such a closure might be, it should not lead us away from care.

1 Foucault on Madness

Three major narratives intertwine within Foucault's text, *Madness and Civilisation*.[1] They concern the political economy of madness,[2] the representation of madness in art and literature, and the relation between madness and science. As we will see in the course of the following expositions, questions can be raised regarding the accuracy of the historical research that lies behind them, and concerning the cogency of both the lines of argumentation and the schemas of interpretation. The important point to grasp, however, is that while specific criticisms may be sustained with respect to some of Foucault's particular statements, what cannot be disputed is the force of his demonstration that the contemporary understanding of mental illness has been shaped by a complex cultural, political, economic and epistemological history. It is a demonstration that completely transcends the geographical restrictions of the research, limited as it is almost entirely to the history of France. As even his fiercest critics will admit, Foucault's book on madness has provided one of the main inspirations for the rethinking, over the last three decades or so, of the nature of insanity.

Foucault's voice is one of the most powerful in that chorus that tells us that to understand the present we must look to the past. We must recognize, however, that access to the past is policed. The normal methods of historical inquiry, and the widespread versions of historical truth, may both function to legitimate the practices of the present. The iconoclastic historian plays a political role.

The Political Economy of Madness

Leprosy was widespread throughout medieval Europe. Foucault's research revealed that 220 lazar houses existed in twelfth-century England and Scotland alone. Throughout Europe at this time there were many thousands of lepers, and extensive provision was made for their exclusion from ordinary society. Attitudes to leprosy were compounded of fear, revulsion and disapprobation, but lepers were nevertheless often well cared for (Midelfort, 1980, p. 253). We have, then, a peculiar phenomenon: lepers were reviled, and excluded from ordinary society; but the places of exile to which the lepers were confined were sufficiently well endowed to provide a regime of care for the victims of the disease. The 'immense fortune represented by the endowments of the lazar houses' (MC, p. 4) testifies to the cultural significance of the leper within the medieval worldview. For Foucault, the leper was *the Other* of the medieval world, a prime source of contamination which was to be treated with respectful fear.

For reasons that are to some extent still obscure, leprosy was much less common by the time of the Renaissance. The practice of social exclusion appears to have had its effect, even if, in contrast with measures taken to control the plague some centuries later,[3] eradication had not been its prime intent. Two questions arise in respect of this reduction in the incidence of leprosy. The first relates to the symbolic function of the leper: what figure is to become the new Other of European society? The second relates to the changes which were bound to take place in what we might call the economy of exclusion. Foucault will show that these two questions are tightly woven together.

The subsisting economic structure, exemplified by the wealth of the lazar houses, was not simply dismantled, with administrative self-congratulation as to a job well done. There was, argues Foucault, a period of disorganized transition extending over some two centuries or more. In part, sufferers from venereal disease inherited both the economic and social legacy of the leper. As Foucault puts it, speaking of the developments in the sixteenth century, 'a new leper is born, who takes the place of the first' (HF, p. 17). But this was neither a smooth nor total transition. While some establishments began to treat syphilitics, in what we might see as the second wave of medicine's institutionally located confrontations with madness,[4] others remained empty for decades. From the middle of the sixteenth century, beginning with the census which François I had undertaken in 1543, the aim of which was to 'remedy the great disorder that exists at present in the lazar houses' (MC, p. 4), a European reorganization and reorientation of the financial infrastructure of exclusion took place. The new isolates were to be the pariahs of non-productivity: the poor, the criminal, the homeless and the mad. How is this new focus to be accounted for?

It is important to set the context. The fifteenth century had been largely a period of economic expansion, and this extended well into the 1600s. But by 1640 this period of expansion was over, and, in France particularly, recession had set in. Among the factors contributing to the complex economic crisis which affected the whole of seventeenth-century Europe, Foucault mentions 'reduction of wages, unemployment, scarcity of coin' (MC, p. 49). To this can be added the cost of such military conflicts as the Thirty Years War, regular famine and plague which affected the state's ability to sustain unprecedentedly high levels of taxation, and demographic contraction which contrasted with the population increases which had at least partly underpinned the previous period of expansion. Against this economic backdrop, the French political system was in a condition of upheaval as the monarchy, in alliance with the rising bourgeoisie, made inroads into the power of the feudal nobility, and built up a pervasive bureaucracy.[5] As Foucault writes, 'This structure proper to the monarchical and bourgeois order of France, contemporary with its organization in absolutist forms, soon extended its network over the whole of France' (MC, p. 41).

Alongside these changes in social structure, the general attitudes and values of European culture were also changing. While it may have been the case, as Weber (1930, p. 177) suggests, that there was a certain celebration of poverty in the medieval mendicant orders, by the beginning of the seventeenth century the position was very different. During the sixteenth and early seventeenth centuries, beggary was anathematized. The poor and homeless were sometimes used as slave labour, in the sewers of Paris, for example, or in the galleys of Spain.[6] At other times, they were expelled from the cities, whether informally or by official decree. The armies of beggars and vagabonds created by the desperate social conditions of Reformation Europe came to be seen as both a political problem, a 'police' matter as Foucault might say, and an affront to the newly developing ethic of work.

As the absolutist states of Europe extended their administrative reach, the Church was effecting both ideological and practical withdrawal from that part of its role which had formerly been concerned with succouring the poor. The teachings of Luther and Calvin, whether received favourably or not, found an echo throughout Europe, as poverty came to be seen as a secular matter. As Foucault explains:

Poverty is no longer held within a dialectic of humiliation and glory, but in a certain relation between disorder and order which surrounds it with guilt. Already, since Luther and Calvin, bearing the marks of eternal punishment, it will become in the world of state-controlled charity complacency in itself and an offence against the good workings of the state.[7] (HF, p. 70)

Economic depression, changed attitudes to poverty, the *de facto* withdrawal of the Church, the emergence of a new work ethic, the administrative expansion of the state, all these factors combine to usher in what Foucault calls 'the age of confinement'. It is, as he notes, 'a phenomenon of European dimensions'. These factors help to explain the workhouse movement in England and the houses of correction – the *Zuchthausern* – in Germany. But Foucault's main focus is on France, and here he identifies a specific moment: the decree of 1656 which founds the General Hospital in Paris.

On the surface, the foundation of the General Hospital appears to be just an administrative regrouping of several pre-existing establishments. Under the king's edict, a variety of establishments were assigned to the poor of Paris. Article eleven of the edict specified that this applied to the destitute 'of both sexes, of all ages and from all localities, of whatever breeding and birth, in whatever state they may be, able-bodied or invalid, sick or convalescent, curable or incurable' (MC, p. 40). On Monday 14 May, 1657, following a second edict which made all forms of begging illegal, the militia began to round up the beggars, thence distributing them around the various buildings of the General Hospital. According to Foucault, this absolutist trawl through the murky waters of destitution netted up to 6,000 people in Paris alone: mad people, libertines, criminals, deviants of all kinds. Poverty, the moral disease of the idle and unproductive, was the necessary and sufficient condition for admission to the hospital. By the time of the Revolution, there were thirty-two such hospitals throughout France.

The constitution of these places makes them truly symbolic, for they were constituted as an entirely autonomous juridical estate. The edict of 1656 speaks of 'stakes, irons, prisons and dungeons' and sets down that no appeal will be allowed with respect to whatever regulations the directors of the General Hospital deem necessary. Thus the inmates of these institutions were both physically and administratively excluded from civil and political society. The insane would find their home in these places apart, not because they were ill, but because they were unproductive.

There is some dispute as to the nature of the hospital regime. Foucault asserts, not incorrectly it would seem, that attempts were made to put the inmates of these institutions to work. It is on this basis, as well as paying due regard to the poor as a potentially politically destabilizing social group, that he can say that confinement was not simply a response to a concatenation of crisis conditions in seventeenth-century Europe. He writes:

> Outside of the periods of crisis, confinement acquired another meaning. Its repressive function was combined with a new use. It was no longer merely a question of confining those out of work, but of giving work to those who had been confined and thus making them contribute to the prosperity of all. The alternation is clear: cheap manpower in the periods of full employment and high salaries; and in periods of unemployment, reabsorption of the idle and social protection against agitation and uprisings. (MC, p. 51)

The symbolic import of the General Hospital rests on the radical exclusion of its inmates. Foucault's history of madness is based on the idea that one can try to document the history of the various forms taken by the social Other, that one can show, by analysing the economic, political and cultural context, how particular groups came to occupy, at various times, the position of the Other. Yet the symbolic equivalence of poverty and leprosy as, in their different epochs, the social Other, was not so firmly fixed. Even if they were often unsuccessful, attempts were made to put the hospital inmates to work. Such attempts hardly attest to the ritual exclusion of the poor from society. It must also be added that this exclusion of the lumpenproletariat from society was nothing like totally effective: poverty was still much in evidence on the streets of Paris, and the politically subversive role of the underclass in eighteenth-century France is well documented (Marx, 1973). The otherness of non-productivity is, then, only partial. Indeed, the General Hospital came to be seen as a place of 'privileged idleness'. In this history of otherness, we are at a transitional stage. But the ethic of work and of contribution to social well-being was crucial. Not only did this somewhat inefficient internment of the unproductive affirm the continuing relevance of the process of exclusion, it was

also out of this heterogeneous process of incarceration that the
mad were gradually crystallized, from the seventeenth century
onwards, as the definitive social Other of the modern period. It
was the inability of the insane to make any ordered contribution
to the economic functioning of the hospitals that helped prepare
the way for the closing of the symbolic transference.[8]

What were these places of confinement really like? Drawing
upon official records and the reports of contemporary witnesses,
Foucault paints a dark picture of filth and suffering. These
hospitals were hard to distinguish from prisons. They were
regimes of punishment and moral condemnation, a fact which
is underlined in Foucault's account of the treatment of venereals
within this system (HF, pp. 97–101). It is hardly surprising,
Foucault comments, that the insane could be found somewhat
indifferently between the prisons and the General Hospital (HF,
p. 129). There was little difference between the two kinds of
institution. Both were concerned with the neutralization of
threats to social order, whether these lay with the animal
ferocity of madness, the violence of crime, or the sedition of
immorality. Tolerance, rehabilitation and cure were not central
items in the absolutist lexicon.

But there was another tradition, one in which medicine and
madness were not foreign to each other. This tradition follows
'the monastic inspiration of custodial care, redemption or rehabilitation as opposed to the sepulchral model of the leprosarium'
(Midelfort, 1980, p. 256). Foucault saw that this humane model
was actually a residue from the past. These practices, contrary
to Midelfort's suggestion that their significance was radically
underestimated, were merely a preamble to internment:

> The world of madness was not uniform in the classical period.
> It would not be false, but partial, to pretend that the mad were
> treated, purely and simply, as prisoners of the authorities.
>
> Some of them have a special status. In Paris, one hospital
> reserves the right to treat poor people who have lost their
> minds. To the extent that it can still be hoped to cure a
> mad person, they may be admitted to the Hôtel-Dieu. The
> customary care will be provided there: Bleedings, purgations,
> and in certain cases, the application of blistering agents and
> baths. This was an old tradition, since this same Hôtel-Dieu
> was already reserving places for the mad in the Middle Ages
> ... But if, after some weeks, the patients have not been cured,
> the men are directed to Bicêtre, the women to La Salpêtrière.

In total, and for the whole of the population of Paris and the surrounding area, there were 74 places reserved for the care of the insane – 74 places constituting the ante-chamber before an internment which precisely signifies the fall away from a world of illness, remedies and eventual cure. (HF, pp. 125-6)

Foucault, then, allows that alongside the massive phenomenon of confinement there existed a social and textual space, whose origins are pre-classical, going right back to Hippocrates, within which a therapeutics of madness is articulated. He will exploit this space to the full, as we shall see in the section of this chapter devoted to madness and science. But the existence of this marginal tradition does not detract from the basic thesis that the origins of confinement are economic, political and cultural, and that it set the scene for the occupation by madness of the vacuum created in the symbolic order brought about by the disappearance of leprosy.

During the 150-year history of the general hospitals in France, poverty was slowly freed from absolute moral condemnation. Industrial growth over this period meant that a labouring class became an economic necessity for national wealth. Poverty could no longer be easily taken as a sign of idleness and promise of social disorder. It became the very opposite of this. As Foucault writes:

In the mercantilist economy, the Pauper, being neither producer nor consumer, had no place: idle, vagabond, unemployed, he belonged only to confinement, a measure by which he was exiled and as it were abstracted from society. With the nascent industry which needs manpower, he once again plays a part in the body of the nation. (MC, p. 230)

The houses of confinement came to be seen as instances of outmoded and economically irrational charity. The secret of wealth would be the exploitation of the poor, not their imprisonment.

Foucault had tried to ask what it was that had bound the inhabitants of the General Hospital into one category. What did the insane, the destitute and the immoral have in common? His answer is that they are outside of the limits of social order as determined by the political and economic conditions of absolutism. Confinement was an ethical response to these conditions, and the play of social forces created a categorial unity which is hard, in the late twentieth century, to understand. As confinement came to an end, at the beginning of the nineteenth century, a new discourse had developed, that of economics. Poverty would now be treated in numerical rather than ethical terms. Both during and after confinement, even though the discourse undergoes fundamental alteration, the understanding and treatment of poverty was an economic and political affair.

Consternation over confinement also emerged in a different way. Even though the attempts to introduce various forms of work into the places of confinement must be deemed to have failed, these attempts did play their part in the gradual differentiation of the mad from the other inmates. It was not merely the widespread requirement of work that established a line of demarcation within the confined population itself, but also the human geography of these places. From the start of the eighteenth century, a swelling protest began to be heard: those that were not mad did not want to have to associate with those that were. As Foucault puts it:

> increasingly, madness becomes the spectre of the internees, the very image of their humiliation, of their reason vanquished and reduced to silence. The day soon comes when Mirabeau recognizes in the shameful promiscuity of madness both a subtle instrument of brutality and the very image of despotism, bestiality triumphant. (MC, pp. 224–5)

The Comte de Mirabeau, a prominent political figure in eighteenth-century France, but one whose excessive lifestyle had resulted in periods of imprisonment, had recognized that madness was in large part an outcome of confinement itself. How are those driven out of society into conditions of utter degradation supposed to behave? How is reason to be retained when all the social supports upon which it rests are knocked away? For the General Hospital and the system of confinement as a whole, madness is not a contingent problem to be coped with by warder and fellow prisoner alike. It is the essence and outcome of the system as a whole, and it is both a terrible irony and a hidden hypocrisy that the rehumanization of its treatment rests on its coming specification as disease. But such, Foucault will tell us again and again throughout his work, is the condition of the human sciences, and such is the relation between power and knowledge: in a process screened behind a veil of objectivity and detachment, epistemological developments function politically to neutralize problems which themselves have arisen out of prior political contexts.

The people of Paris, especially those living close to the fortress walls of Bicêtre and La Salpêtrière, may not have had Foucault's understanding of how madness might spread. But they knew that all was not well. What Foucault terms 'the Great Fear' arose in the middle of the eighteenth century. The people were afraid of a mysterious disease that originated, it was said, from the houses of confinement. As Foucault explains, devoting a whole chapter to the topic, this is a very complex reaction to the system of confinement. First, it is a condemnation of confinement as a practice of stagnation which is bound to promote disease. Even by the middle of the eighteenth century, there was a general recognition that change rather than immobility was the immanent condition of the social world. Thus the social context adds its own emphasis to nature's abhorrence of stagnancy. Second, it is a cry for protection: confinement has created images of unpredictable violence and disruptive frenzy. The typical mad person is no longer the fool but the raving lunatic. Third, it is a call for the medical profession whose practitioners will arrive as sentinels rather than as kindly and concerned humanitarians.

Disturbingly, however, the general significance of confinement does not exhaust itself on the negative plane. For in this veritable moral panic, a new relationship emerges; the exclusionary excesses of confinement have their effect outside the fortress walls in a new connection between fear and desire. Foucault writes:

> Sadism is not a name finally given to a practice as old as Eros; it is a massive cultural fact which appeared precisely at the end of the eighteenth century, and which constitutes one of the greatest conversions of Western imagination: unreason transformed into delirium of the heart, madness of desire, the insane dialogue of love and death in the limitless presumption of appetite. Sadism appears at the very moment that unreason, confined for over a century and reduced to silence, reappears. (MC, p. 210)

As a political and economic failure, confinement was bound to come to an end. But it had fashioned new images of madness, both inside and outside its walls. It is in this context, Foucault tells us, that we must understand the interventions of Pinel and Tuke. The French physician, Philippe Pinel, became head of

Bicêtre in 1793, and both there and at La Salpêtrière, he is widely credited with introducing a more humane regime for the insane. The Englishman, Samuel Tuke, founded the Retreat at York, a place where insanity could be met and overcome in an environment of religion, calm and contemplation. These men, whom the standard histories of psychiatric medicine portray in triumphalist terms as the modern originators of the mental hospital, form a part of the armature of power. This applies in a double sense. First of all, as we have seen, the object of their attention, i.e. the condition of insanity itself, was a product of the flows of historical change and altering sociopolitical exigency. Their objectifying, humanizing and medicalizing treatment of the condition of insanity, however, requires the concealment of its newly stigmatized recent past. Secondly, the therapeutic treatment begun by those such as Pinel and Tuke located the responsibility for the condition of insanity within the sufferers themselves, a shift of responsibility which constitutes the second precondition of the successful development of the nascent science of mental health.

It is reported that Pinel himself opened the gates of Bicêtre in 1794. This may not actually be true.[9] But what, for Foucault, is beyond doubt is that Pinel did not liberate the insane in any real sense:

> The asylum of the age of positivism, which it is Pinel's glory to have founded, is not a free realm of observation, diagnosis and therapeutics; it is a juridical space where one is accused, judged and condemned, and from which one is never released except ... by remorse.[10]

The medicalization of madness, its transformation of madness into mental illness, may have defused the images of depravity which haunted the medical horizon of the nineteenth century, and may even have associated madness and innocence in the modern world, as, for example, insanity becomes a defence which can be pleaded in criminal trials. But the asylum itself was a regime of automatic guilt. Its successful products are remorseful, and eager to return to an orderly working life in the capitalist world.

We have been centrally concerned with the economic and political preconditions of a newly emerging category of social being, the mental patient. Confinement was an invention of the absolutist state, a consequence of its spreading power and bureaucratic control. But the authorities had little control over the figures which were nurtured by this system. This is what makes the administrative continuity between the exclusion of lepers and the confinement of the socially undesirable so poignant. It matters little that most of the general hospitals were not disused leprosaria. The point is that the administrative and financial continuity does exist, even if only marginally. Thus the continuity can operate as an arresting footnote to the displacement of the leper colony by the house of confinement as the place of the Other. Inside this new purgatory, changes were taking place which were never envisaged. New beasts of the imagination were released into the outside world, and these had to be controlled. The advent of new values, rooted in economic and political change, and expressed by the emerging disciplines of economics, medicine and psychology, functions, together with many other techniques, to maintain the docile workforce of which Foucault will tell us much more in his later work, *Discipline and Punish*.

The lesson of the historical narrative, drawn by Roland Barthes in an early review of Foucault's text, is that

the fundamental acts of human life are historical objects ... we must redefine, in each case, according to each society observed, facts reputed to be natural by reason of their physical character. (Barthes, 1972, p. 163)

The medical objectification of madness deprives it of its material history and hence of a crucial aspect of its 'truth'. In order to discover other facets of this 'truth', to find, in a realm apart from that of social power, what the essence of madness is, Foucault looked to its representation in painting and literature. Perhaps here one could find a clue to the basic nature of madness, perhaps one could hope to see it in a pure representation uncorrupted by historical machination. It was a quest which he would later denounce, perhaps partly as a result of Derrida's critique. But this is to anticipate. For the moment we should just see what Foucault thought himself to have found.

Madness in Art and Literature

There is 'a great line of cleavage in the Western experience of madness'.[11] On the one hand, madness is inexplicable and

holds out the threat of dark and unknown regions. On the
other hand, madness is explicable; it is foolishness and illusion,
a condition of error which has some prior cause. The line of
cleavage, then, is between the Other and the Same, between
the transcendental and the empirical, between the sublime and
the mundane, between fear and control, and ultimately perhaps
between the bright hope of difference and the monotony of
bourgeois reason. In Foucault's view, the depiction of madness
by Renaissance painters was concerned with the fantastic and
terrible territory of the Other, while the writers of this period
were already treating madness as a matter of this-worldly significance. Foucault writes:

> On one side, Bosch, Brueghel, Thierry Bouts, Dürer, and the
> pervading silence of the image. It is in this space of pure vision
> that madness will display its powers ... in that space, madness
> possesses a primitive force of revelation ...
>   On the other side, with Brant, with Erasmus, and with the
> whole humanist tradition, madness is set within the universe
> of discourse. There it is refined ... and disarmed. (HF, pp.
> 38–9)

For Foucault, this opposition between cosmic revelation and
critical morality is virtually resolved by the end of the Renaissance:
discursive domestication had eclipsed the fantasies of the figural.
From that point forward, only the occasional murmurings of a
de Sade, or the visionary explorations of a Goya, would hint
that the opposition had not really been destroyed, but that it
had been overlaid and hidden by a compact between science
and morality.

How well does this thesis stand up to close examination? As we
will see, Foucault's interpretations are, to say the least, stretched.
Many of the paintings considered by him show madness not to
possess a 'primitive force of revelation', but rather to pose and
to be a form and threat within *this* world. While, as we will
see, a close analysis of the paintings concerned will lead us to
dispute his specific interpretation of art in the Renaissance era.
This will actually turn out to be a state of affairs that is in accord
with the general spirit of Foucault's overall inquiry. The painters
are prepared to face the ineffaceable reality of madness, to live
with its constant presence, to allow that some things are beyond
understanding. They do not point to what madness might be in
its entirely separate realm, but rather to what madness can do

within this world of ours; a world of which madness has to be acknowledged as a part. Their works do not immediately testify to a hope for the excision of madness from the social world. For the writers, on the other hand, madness can be understood, which is the first step towards its eradication, its exclusion from the social realm.

Let us consider first the paintings to which Foucault refers. There are six Renaissance paintings which concern Foucault particularly. They are *The Cure of Madness*, *The Ship of Fools* and *The Temptation of St Anthony* by Hieronymus Bosch; *The Triumph of Death* and *Dulle Griet* by Pieter Brueghel; and *Horsemen of the Apocalypse* by Dürer.

Foucault does not discuss *The Cure of Madness* in any detail. The picture shows the ludicrous figure of a surgeon, with the 'funnel of wisdom' on his head, removing a wild flower from the open-eyed skull of a portly burgher.

Two figures appear to the side of this primitive trepanation: a monk holding a jug of wine seems to approve of the proceedings, while a nun, with a book on her head, stares vacuously into the distance. This circular picture is set within a dark ornamented rectangle in which the following words are boldly and exquisitely inscribed: 'Meester snijt die Keije ras Mijne Name is Lubbert das' ('Master, cut out the stones. My name is gelded dog'). The picture is a double commentary on madness: it refers to the absurd and mad thought that the sin and disorder of the human condition can be excised by physical means, and it attests to the inadequacy of religious writ in dealing with the dark side of the psyche. In other words, the picture might be taken as alluding to the territory of the Other, but, more centrally, it satirizes the vanity of thinking that its powers might be exorcised. What the picture does not do is present a pure vision of madness. Madness is present here only by allusion, and the reference is to the madness of misbegotten brain surgery as much as to the condition of the patient.

Foucault has three points to make about Bosch's *Ship of Fools*: first that it is a representation of Sebastian Brant's poem of the same name, and that both of these works emerge from a fifteenth-century sensibility to the relation between madness and embarkation; second that the tree which forms the mast in Bosch's picture is 'the forbidden tree, the tree of promised immortality and of sin [which] has been uprooted and now forms the mast of the *Ship of Fools*' (MC, p. 22); and, third, that the lust and gluttony of the mad crew represent a 'false happiness [which] is the diabolical triumph of the Antichrist' (MC, p. 22). Each of these assertions may be questioned.

First, it is mere surmise that Bosch had Brant's poem in mind when doing this painting (Gibson, 1973, p. 41). Furthermore, the 'precise' relation which Foucault finds between the picture and the canto of Brant's poem titled 'Of gluttony and feasting' is revealed, on close inspection, to be somewhat problematic. Brant's condemnation of gluttony is backed up by extensive references to stories from the Bible. If such stories are represented in Bosch's picture (beyond the presence of a monk and at least one nun, whose role can be explained by supposing that part of Bosch's objective was to expose the licentiousness which existed within the contemporary monastic and religious orders), they are obscure to modern eyes. Additionally there is very little sense in Bosch's painting of the embarkation, of journeying to places unknown, of the mysteries of navigation. The painting is, in fact, remarkably static. It is a portrayal of the human condition which lacks clear reference to the realm of the transcendental. It is, in other words, a cautionary painting; discourse rather than figure, in Foucault's scheme of things. Even though the work may be seen as an exercise in moralizing, however, there is no sense of madness tamed or about to be tamed within the frame.

On the second point, that the mast of the boat in Bosch's picture is 'without a doubt' the fabled tree of knowledge from the Garden of Eden, two things should be noted. First, the reference may well have been to the may tree of popular spring festivals, a figure which signified a certain general moral freedom. Second, Foucault's reference to the 'tree of immortality' is somewhat strange, for the tree of knowledge of good and evil in the Garden of Eden was precisely a tree of mortality, a tree whose fruit meant the end of paradise and the advent of the degenerative human life cycle which will thenceforth turn incessantly from birth to death. There were, of course, two trees in the Garden. The other tree, the tree of life, was not forbidden. It was only after Adam and Eve succumbed to the temptation of the serpent, and knew evil, that God banished them from paradise so that they would not be able to eat from the tree of immortality. In any event, if the tree in Bosch's picture is indeed the tree of knowledge, it is further confirmation that Bosch's picture is angled against the transcendental and that it lacks the aspiration to penetrate the territory of the Other.

With regard to the last assertion, that the picture alludes to 'the false happiness [which] is the diabolical triumph of the

Antichrist', there is, again, a certain imprecision in Foucault's rhetoric. The picture actually illustrates the path to that triumph, showing the kind of life that leads to the devil's victory at the Last Judgement. Even then the victory of the diabolical is not presented by Bosch as absolute. In his *Last Judgement* triptych, the devil triumphant in the central panel remains counterposed to the vision of beauty and peace presented by the last panel. Overall, *The Ship of Fools* is a satire upon and complaint against human frailties and hypocrisies. But it lacks the allusion to and the invocation of unknown powers which would make it an ideal support for Foucault's thesis of a developing split between the pictorial illustration of otherness and the secular pedogogy of contemporary writing.

Foucault's discussion of Bosch's *Temptation of St Anthony*[12] is a little fuller than his commentary on *The Ship of Fools*. It reads as follows:

What assails the hermit's tranquillity is not objects of desire, but these hermetic, demented forms which have risen from a dream, and remain silent and furtive on the surface of a world. In the Lisbon *Temptation*, facing St Anthony sits one of these figures born of madness, of its solitude, of its penitence, of its privations; a wan smile lights this bodiless face, the pure presence of anxiety in the form of an agile grimace. Now it is exactly this nightmare silhouette that is at once the subject and object of the temptation; it is this figure which fascinates the gaze of the ascetic – both are prisoners of a kind of mirror interrogation, which remains unanswered in a silence inhabited only by the monstrous swarm that surrounds them ... The freedom, however frightening, of his dreams, the hallucinations of his madness, have more power of attraction for fifteenth-century man than the desirable reality of the flesh. (MC, pp. 20–1)

It is difficult to accept this interpretation which distinguishes between hallucinations of madness and desires of the flesh. St Anthony is said to have lived twenty years in the desert, during which time he faced many temptations. The point here is that St Anthony was out of the world and was tempted by the world, a world no doubt fabulously embroidered by the imagination. But this world nevertheless.

What Bosch portrays is the ugly disorder of a mad world. If his art may be seen as counter-praxis, it is because he was ahead of the political calendar of madness as described by Foucault. His work assimilates madness and humanity. His response to this diagnosis is moral and religious: self-discipline and communion with God. For Bosch, the realm of the Other is not the place of madness, but rather the site of perpetual peace and eternal salvation. But his work confirms that there was never for him the question of permanently excising madness from the world. For Bosch, madness is a part of all of us.

Brueghel painted the *Dulle Griet* and *The Triumph of Death* at about the same time, probably in 1562. To contemplate these works, side by side, as it were, is to witness a profound ambiguity. But it is not the ambiguity between otherness and morality which Foucault describes.

On the one hand, *The Triumph of Death* depicts the skeletal soldiers of Thanatos reaping their grim harvest. Struggle is useless against their power: a pilgrim lies unresisting while a clothed but fleshless fiend cuts his throat; a fool crawls under a table; the emperor does nothing but fondle the flank of a soldier of death whose spider-leg arms reach into his coffers. Images of death, panic and catastrophe abound as the death-cull is carried out in a display of macabre efficiency. This is Brueghel's rendering of the end, of the zero-point of existence, of the margin between the sublime and the mundane, between the earth and the Other. On the other hand, the *Dulle Griet* is a presentation of competing forces. While unspeakable monsters, drawn from the depths of hell, represent the various sins, the picture is dominated by 'mad Meg'. Her loot is carried on an arm which ends in a metal gauntlet. She wears armour. Her right hand carries a sword with which she will defend her earthly acquisitions. She is ready to do battle with the demons of hell because she knows that this life is all that there is. She will triumph in the temporal, secured from the nameless Other by the frontier of death. The ambiguity, then, is between death as the end of hope and death as the line which holds otherness back, as, in other words, guarantor of hope. It is resolved with the realization that death is the end of transcendental hope but the ground of hope in the temporal sphere. Like Bosch, Brueghel would locate unreason firmly in this world.

Foucault's insistence on Bosch and Brueghel's association of unreason and the Other is, then, hard to accept. The more compelling view is that the art of Bosch and Brueghel anticipates the understanding of unreason as a problem which besets this world. That it was to be dissolved by an alliance of the forces of

politics and rationality, would, however, have come as a surprise
to them. For their work intimates that the desperate condition
of the world is that madness has always been here, and that it
will remain so for all time.

Nor does the vision of Albrecht Dürer negate this minor
correction of Foucault's view. Foucault wrote:

> It is enough to look at Dürer's *Horsemen of the Apocalypse*,
> sent by God Himself: these are no angels of triumph and
> reconciliation; these are no heralds of serene justice, but the
> dishevelled warriors of a mad vengeance. The world sinks into
> a universal Fury. Victory is neither God's nor the Devil's: it
> belongs to Madness. (MC, p. 23)

But it is *not* enough to look at this single woodcut, a part of a
series illustrating the Book of Revelation, otherwise known as
the Apocalypse.

As the text of Revelation makes clear, and as the whole series
of Dürer's woodcuts makes exceedingly plain, the Apocalypse
is part of a process of cleansing the human realm. The end of
the process is described in Revelation, Chapter XXII:

> And he shewed me a pure river of water of life, clear as crystal,
> proceeding out of the throne of God and of the Lamb. In the
> midst of the street of it, and on either side of the river, was
> there the tree of life, which bare twelve manner of fruits, and
> yielded her fruit every month; and the leaves of the tree were
> for the healing of the nations. And there shall be no more
> curses.

John's vision is perfectly consonant with the scourging and
apocalyptic aspirations of the French absolutist state: the sinners
are cast into houses of confinement, and when unreason is
banished from the land, the new Jerusalem will be signified by
the white walls of the mental hospital. In short, the art which
Foucault sees as transgressing the coming temporalization of
unreason does not really do this. It concedes, and perhaps in a
certain sense celebrates, the existence of madness and unreason
in *this world*. It does not, except arguably in Dürer's case,
anticipate that madness might be seen as a temporal problem
to be solved. But it does warn of its dangers and depict its
power. In one sense, then, such salutory illustrations may have
solicited our complicity in all those projects which promised that

such dangers can be removed. Certainly the difference between Renaissance painting and Renaissance writing was pivotal. But the difference was not that between depiction of otherness and denial of otherness. It was between the depiction of a disordered world and the distant promise of control.

For Foucault, the philosophy and literature of the Renaissance accorded a certain privilege to madness. Folly held pride of place in the catalogue of human weaknesses. It held this place because of the ambiguity and precariousness afflicting all forms of human endeavour. This instability can be demonstrated by considering the questions of knowledge and ambition. What might have been thought about the philosopher's quest for knowledge? As exemplified by the search for the philosopher's stone which would transmute base metal into gold, and as parodied by Erasmus who writes of demented dance-steps performed by scholars of all kinds, the detachment of learning from the practical world of experience may appear deeply unreasonable. Nevertheless, knowledge, abstraction and wisdom are clearly related. As for the question of ambition, is it not a strange thing to look at oneself in a mirror and to see what is not there, to presume to behold what one could be rather than what one is? This is close to illusion, even delusion. Knowledge and ambition, or perhaps we should say science and politics, these are forces which will propel the world into the next era. Yet they are intimately connected to the rejection of the world as it is.

Madness is a constant threat for the Renaissance. It is the punishment and condition of excess: too much imagination, desperate passion, the over-zealous pursuit of seemingly reasonable ideals. Madness is the human condition beyond Aristotle's Golden Mean, an ontological possibility to be guarded against. This is what Foucault means when he says that madness is inscribed within 'a completely moral universe [in which] evil is not punishment or the end of time, but only fault and flaw' (MC, p. 27). But madness, even though coming to be seen as all too human, within the literary sensibility of the time, still, for Foucault, meant that a limit had been crossed without possibility of return. The last great works that attest to the finality of madness in this epoch are, Foucault suggests, those of Shakespeare and Cervantes. They are seen as the last representatives of a literary sensibility which combines both madness as otherness and madness as willed downfall. Foucault's insight here can be sharpened by considering two passages, one from *Don Quixote* and the other from *King Lear*, neither of which does he himself discuss. In *Don Quixote*, Cervantes tells of a madman who is aware of his condition as an achievement:

> There was a madman in Seville who was taken with the oddest and craziest notion that ever a madman had in all the world. It was this: he made a tube out of a cane, sharpened at the one end, and catching a dog, in the street or elsewhere, he would hold down one of its hind legs with one foot and lift the other one up with his hand. Next, fitting his tube to the right place, he would blow into it as best he could, till he had made the dog round as a ball. Then holding it up in this way, he would give it a couple of slaps on the belly and let it go, saying to the bystanders – and there were always plenty: 'Your worships will perhaps be thinking it is an easy thing to blow up a dog?' (Cervantes, p. 468)

The final sentence of Cervantes' story points to the involvement of the will in madness, and it is, in fact, an ambiguous involvement: indeterminate between the effort of will required to become mad, and the effort of will required to sustain a life lived within the territory of the Other.

King Lear, on the other hand, emphasizes the social causation of madness. Consider the scene on the heath, in front of the hovel, with Edgar disguised as the madman, Tom:

> Edgar: Who gives any thing to poor Tom, whom the foul fiend hath led through fire, and through flame, through ford and whirlpool, o'er bog and quagmire; that hath laid knives under his pillow, and halters in his pew, set ratsbane by his porridge, made him proud of heart to ride on a bay trotting-horse over four-inch'd bridges, to course his own shadow for a traitor. Bless thy five wits! Tom's a-cold. O! do de, do de, do de. Bless thee from whirlwinds, star-blasting and taking! Do poor Tom some charity, whom the foul fiend vexes. There could I have him now, and there, and there again, and there.
>
> Lear: What! has his daughters brought him to this pass? ...
>
> Kent: He hath no daughters, Sir.
>
> Lear: Death, traitor! nothing could have subdued nature to such a lowness but his unkind daughters.

Like Cervantes' madman of Seville, Lear has a certain recognition of the causes of madness, and they are social causes.
But even while understanding madness, Lear remains resigned
to it as a natural condition, a personal destiny which could not
be turned aside.

As represented by Cervantes and Shakespeare, the literary
perception of madness in the post-Renaissance is equivocal. In
part, it speaks of madness, folly, a certain social indiscipline, if
you will, as an ordinary feature of a world characterized by the
constant threat of disorder. On the other side, however, it looks
forward, with a growing awareness, to a time when all aspects
of social behaviour will have their explanation and, if necessary,
their remedy.

The intimate connection between madness and the will, and
between madness and society, will soon slip from recognition
as madness comes in the post-Renaissance to be defined purely
as error and irresponsibility. It will no longer be irredeemable.
Its worldly truth will have changed, not because of an alteration
in the nature of madness, but because of a change in the order of
the world. The emblem of madness will soon no longer be the
ship which takes lost souls on a journey into the unknown, but a
place of correction whether hospital or prison: the madhouse.

For Foucault, 200 years of silence follow the works of Cervantes
and Shakespeare. European madness is rendered mute behind
fortress walls. Then, alongside the expressive mythology of
Pinel's gesture of liberation, there arise, at the very edge
of art and literature, words and images of a new order of
disturbance. The two figures who reinsert madness into the
cultural imagination of the early nineteenth century are Goya
and the Marquis de Sade. These men are, for Foucault, of
epochal significance.

A number of Goya's works are mentioned in passing. None is
subjected to thorough analysis. Pursuing a rigorous dilettantism,
Foucault sketches a complex thesis:

> Goya's forms are born out of nothing ... The *Disparates* are
> without landscape, without walls, without setting ... All that
> is present is the most internal, and at the same time the
> most savagely free, of forces: the power which hacks apart
> the bodies in the *Gran Disparate*, which breaks free and
> assaults our eyes in the *Raging Madness* ... this is no longer
> the madness of the *Caprichos* ... this is a madness beneath the
> mask.[13]

He is telling us, then, of two series of works: the *Caprichos* and the *Disparates*. The former are a series of etchings and aquatints done by Goya in 1797 and 1798. The original frontispiece to this series bore the title '*Ydioma universal*', the universal language. One can dispute what this title might signify. Goya himself claimed that he wished to establish the right of the artist to select from all that nature provides, and further to emphasize that the artist was to be understood as a critical commentator on this multiplicity, rather than a mere recorder. Foucault reads its significance rather differently, seeing Goya's reference to the universal as betokening a renewed interest in the ensemble of reason *and* unreason. The images tend to support Foucault. Of particular interest is *Caprichos* no. 43. This shows Goya himself asleep across a desk upon which his pen and papers are strewn; bats and owls converge on the sleeping figure from out of the darkness, and inscribed on the side of the desk are the words 'El sueño de la razon produce monstruos' ['The dream of reason brings forth monsters']. The meaning, for Foucault, could not be clearer: the sleep of unreason is at an end.

But *Los Caprichos* are not so threatening. They are premissed on the describability of madness. Madness here is nightmare. As such, it presents no insuperable threat to the open eyes of the rational mind. It can be overcome. As Foucault argues, the language of *Los Caprichos* 'is close to the world of Pinel' (MC, p. 279). The series of lithographs known as the *Disparates* (*El Disparate* was the contemporary Spanish nickname for Bosch!), or the *Proverbs* as they are known in English, were produced some twenty years later. These works do not contain visions of night monsters as much as expressions of non-being, of meaninglessness, of a human species without ground or recourse. *The Witches' Sabbath*, an oil painting which Goya began shortly after completing the *Disparates*, is a devastating expression of darkness, a depiction of 'glances shot from nowhere and staring at nothing' (MC, p. 281). These later works are much more disturbing. Their effect is to disorient and diminish the rational mind, and to do this by summoning up powers which remain outside of ordinary comprehension. The *Disparates* tell us that try as we might, we will never be able fully to exorcise the ghosts of otherness.

Goya's two-step into darkness is, according to Foucault, precisely duplicated by de Sade. Just as Goya's *Caprichos* illuminate the horror of natural multiplicity, so in de Sade's *Justine* we are presented with the vicissitudes of a hydra-headed desire which, after all, was given to humankind by nature itself. But this is just the first stage, a gigantic pastiche upon Rousseau's state of nature, as Foucault remarks ironically (MC, p. 283). With *Juliette* we turn to the nameless and shapeless force, perhaps alluded to in the second of the *Disparates*, entitled *Folly of Fear*, which is sovereign over nature: a domination over nature 'in a total absence of proportion and community' (MC, p. 284). This last phrase of Foucault's might just as easily have referred to Goya's *The Witches' Sabbath*. The pure horror of nothingness presented by that picture repeats the terrible arbitrariness of murder and mutilating gratification depicted in *Juliette*.

Foucault ends this narrative by evoking Nietzsche, Artaud and Van Gogh. Their message, like the lessons of de Sade and Goya, is that all is without foundation. God is dead. All is permitted. The pretensions of reason are shattered to hell. From Goya's portrayal of terrified citizens facing the firing squad to the mythical bridge of skulls in Cambodia, the contours of humanity are traced in demented lines on human skin. But, and this is the worst of it, there is neither support nor ground for complaint. Unreason is the unutterable depth of an absolute lack.

Foucault's view of the Renaissance paintings which we have discussed is that they communicate something approaching a vision of otherness. We have seen that this interpretation of these works is difficult to sustain. In a slight adjustment of Foucault's thesis here, it has been shown that these works depict the threat of madness and disorder in our world. The works of Bosch and the others do not treat madness as eradicable, but rather as an existential companion and concomitant of reason. They testify to the medieval recognition that unreason and reason are inseparable. The literature of the Renaissance, however, begins to seek an understanding of madness. Even if writers like Erasmus, Cervantes and Shakespeare recognize that madness has causes, in the will or in the social context, they still tend to treat it as an irredeemable condition of human existence. By the beginning of the nineteenth century, that acceptance of unreason as an inevitable part of the human condition no longer obtained. By this time, only the occasional insights of alienated artists like Goya or de Sade testified that the arrogant claims of a neutralizing science might be false, and that, in spite of the claims of medicine and psychology, the connection between reason and unreason would never be broken.

Madness and Science

Alongside the political and economic processes leading to the emergence of mental illness as a seemingly solid category of a well-established branch of knowledge, and alongside the trail of a counter-cultural art and literature which undulates from the sublime through moralism and thence to visions of perversion and fear, there is a third narrative on madness. This narrative is concerned with those conceptions specific to insanity. While the political economy of madness is founded on the indiscriminate collection of various forms of non-productivity, and while art and literature have, at the margins, been concerned with unreason *tout court*, there have been those concerned with madness as object. They have not been concerned with it as a politico-economic problem, nor as a conduit to the heart of the profoundest cultural hermeneutic, but as a phenomenon to be methodically observed, rigorously understood and thence inserted into a network of effective therapeutic practices.

It has been often observed that Foucault writes against the standard form of scientific histories which would speak of discoveries and of advances in the understanding of things. However, although his work makes such histories inadequate, it does not vitiate them entirely. They too have a story to tell, even if their narratives have been for too long woefully ignorant of the political and hermeneutic aspects of their subject material.

For Foucault, knowledge of any 'object' is never a simple matter. No matter how coherent and restricted a science may be, 'obscure forms of conciousness – practical, mythic, moral – will always revolve around it' (HF, p. 181). It may be said that this is a question of plural perspectives, that 'the same thing' can always be seen from different points of view. Madness, however, seems to present something rather more extreme. It is here, perhaps, that one finds an essential incoherence which operates not at the level of perspectival difference, but rather in the very structures of the phenomenon. Foucault thus argues that the history of madness presents, behind the disguise of historical difference, disarticulated concatenations of four quite specific and eternally irreducible (HF, p. 182) forms of consciousness of madness.

The first of these is referred to as 'a critical consciousness of madness'. In the face of the perceived aberrations of mad conduct, such a consciousness neither seeks to define its concepts nor to understand its own precariousness. It has only an ungrounded confidence in its own reason, and from that position seeks only to condemn. But, as Foucault points out, this primitive opposition is reversible. Who is to say where reason lies in such a case? Might not such an opposition, Foucault asks, be a 'stratagem of madness itself' (HF, p. 182)? But it is not the case that such a rhetorical question signals denunciation, for in the very reversibility of reason and madness is grounded the possibility of a dialogue between judgement and heedless desire. Alas, Foucault seems to say, it also grounds the possibility of fundamental social division.

It is this latter possibility which forms the second type of consciousness, what Foucault calls, 'a practical consciousness of madness'. What is in question here is the social group with powers of exclusion which are based on the canon of normative obedience. In this context, madness is willed and culpable infraction. It illustrates what is forbidden. It exemplifies the continued presence of the power to transgress. It must be silenced. No dialogue is possible. The menace of madness is dealt with through rites of exclusion which find their legitimation in the homogeneity of the rules of reason and the norms of the social group. It is, if you will, the unacceptable face of the sacred.[14]

The third form of consciousness of madness is 'an enunciative consciousness of madness'. It seems to be the simplest form. It is the consciousness which operates when someone is declared mad. As Foucault remarks, there is no question here of exclusion, simply of identifying a substantive instance of madness. But this is not pure identification; there is also a judgement involved, and this is the implied judgement that whosoever declares someone to be mad is sane.

From the mundane objectification of madness exemplified by the average citizen who says, in a matter-of-fact kind of way, that this or that person is mad, we move to the last form of consciousness of madness: 'an analytic consciousness of madness'. Here madness becomes an object of knowledge, an arena for science.

Each of these forms of consciousness is self-sufficient, but nevertheless they are solidary with each other. But, both separately and together, they fail to *know* madness. Although faced with the deployment of the main strategies of the complex consciousness of madness, i.e. the strategies of judgement, rejection, recognition and analysis, madness still eludes capture by any of the forms of reason, whether social, moral, legal, practical or scientific. It is in this context that Foucault's extended account of therapeutics and classification of classical[15] madness must be understood. The categorical framework of classical alienism is the detritus of an impossible science, and the symbol of enlightenment arrogance. Foucault's book as a whole contains the implicit but powerful message that the arrogance and impossibility remain to the present day.

How then was madness treated in the classical age, in those ante-chambers of confinement, like the Hôtel-Dieu, where there existed marginal ideas of therapy and cure? The basic thing to grasp, Foucault suggests, is that during this age of confinement the second and third forms of consciousness were dominant. Knowledge of madness from the seventeenth through to the nineteenth centuries arose out of a certain priority given to recognition, to reading its signs. The classical semiotic of madness is perfectly consonant with the practice of confinement. It is based on a double reading. On the one hand the signs of madness are produced by a disorder of individual reason due to excessive passion or uncontrolled delirium. On the other hand these signs are due to particular bodily conditions which could be classified and separated one from another, just as the botanist would distinguish between different species of plant (HF, p. 206). The overall situation is made even more complex because rather ill-defined notions of body and soul were intertwined in general conceptions of the human condition. What it amounts to is that while there were classifications of madness in the classical age, and while there were medical conceptions of bodily disorder producing aberrations of the mind, there was not a conception of mental illness during this time. Thus the various treatments that were practised, like forced baths and the use of emetics, derived in part from a dimly perceived inheritance from the past and in part from the location of newly emerging medical groupings within an apparatus of power. Even though the process may not have been a conscious one, the treatment of madness by 'doctors' involved an application of old methods which were based on a semiotic of surfaces and resemblances[16] and on an anthropology of body and soul. The effective outcome of this was to be the desacralization of madness and the cementing of the nexus between reason and power. The powerful strictures of a moral discipline addressed imbalances of the soul; the boundlessly self-confident treatments of a nascent medical science dealt with the body; and this double confidence in the power of knowledge caused madness to be perceived as pathology, as a problem to be overcome and even entirely banished from the human realm.

It is instructive to consider some of the classifications of madness and to see how the treatments correspond to this surface semiotic and to the idea of interanimation between body and soul. Foucault discusses four basic types of madness: melancholia, mania, hysteria and hypochondria. Melancholia is seen to be the result of heavy and dark viscosity of bodily waters; mania is a sign of dryness with the body seen as a parched desert; hysteria indicates over-activity of the nervous fibres; hypochondria results from weakness of these fibres. All these forms of madness take the sufferer into a world of delirious error or passionate excess: madness as a condition of the soul is accounted for, at least in part, by the condition of the body. Thus the early therapeutics of madness may be arranged under four headings: purification, immersion, regulation of movement, and consolidation. The idea of purification is founded on the notion of madness as contamination: the dark, viscous blood of the melancholic is unclean, and its replacement by light, clear blood will produce much improvement; soap and 'soapy products' may be used to advantage. Water may be used to purify and rehydrate the maniac. The hysteric's movements should be carefully regulated; if the nervous fibres are excited, then silence and stillness may be the appropriate treatment. If these same fibres are rigid, then walking, running, even horseback riding may re-establish their natural mobility. If the hypochondriac's condition derives from weakness, then consolidation of bodily strength and fibrous health may be produced by, for example, large daily doses of iron. Underlying these conceptions and treatments is the idea of a natural balance between body and soul. There is a harmony to be found between the passions of the mind and the fluids, fibres and vapours of the body. The treatment of madness will seek to restore this harmony.

But classical conceptions of madness are not only founded on a surface naturalism, there is also a certain logic: the logic of delirium. The phenomenon of dreaming can provide a means whereby we can understand it. A dream may be absurd, but this does not mean that the dreamer is mad. It is only when the dream is taken for reality, when its logic is pursued in the waking world, that madness is present. Foucault is understandably disturbed that the madness of delirium seems only to reside in the acceptance of a false premiss. Once the premiss is accepted, the logic of madness and that of normality are identical. So who is to rule on the correctness or otherwise of the premiss? How in these circumstances can the specification of madness by fiat be avoided? As Foucault points out the philosophy and medicine of madness are quite complicit with the political structure of confinement and exclusion.

The genealogical connections between the classical conceptions of madness and twentieth-century views are, for Foucault, reasonably clear. The conceptual universe defined by the impassioned mind and the abnormal body will shift and develop to produce a positivistic concept of mental illness and a physiologically grounded treatment regime of drugs and electric shocks. At an angle to this, the notion of delirium, with its logic and language, will finally produce Freud and the 'talking cure'. What is clear from this is that any reading of classical conceptions of madness which would treat them as part of the developing story of mainstream scientific psychiatry would be partial almost to the level of untruth. The situation is made even more complex by the development of a moral sensibility. Certain kinds of madness, principally hysteria and hypochondria, come to be seen as the consequence of moral fault. On the topic of hysteria, Foucault has this to say:

> [Hysteria] attacks more women than men, because they have a more delicate, less firm constitution, because they lead a softer life, and because they are accustomed to the luxuries and commodities of life and not to suffering. And already ... this spatial density yields one of its meanings: it is also a moral density; the resistance of the organs to the disordered penetration of the spirits is perhaps one and the same thing as that strength of soul which keeps the thoughts and the desires in order. (MC, p. 149)

What this passage points to is the element of judgement in the diagnosis of madness; a life of luxury finds its reward in a deterioration of mind and body – at least, such was a common judgement as the eighteenth century draws to a close.

At the beginning of the nineteenth century, then, the arrangement of the forms of consciousness of madness was quite specific: only distant echoes of the relation between reason and its other remain; the field as a whole is defined in terms of the necessity of legal deprivation of subjecthood, anatomo-neurological conceptions of somatic disorder, and morally judgemental inculcation of self-discipline and sober habits. For Foucault, the modern asylum, which replaces the houses of confinement, is the expression of a new form of repression. The medical personality is a crucial figure in a new drama scripted in terms of psychiatric science and the seemingly universal language of reasonable behaviour.

Within the terms of the accepted structure of reasonable conduct (which have changed little between then and now), Anne Digby (1985) and others (Sedgwick, 1982; Merquior, 1985) are not obviously wrong to question Foucault's depiction of this new asylum as repressive. But the accusation of repression goes much deeper than the level at which questions of empirical and historical detail can settle such argument. What is at issue in Foucault's implicit accusation of repression is precisely the accepted structure of reasonable behaviour itself, because the practices of the asylum and their defence as non-repressive even in the 1980s show just how exclusive and confident the language of reason has become: *there is no system of reasonable behaviour possible other than the one which is our own.* The phenomenon of madness might have been once the occasion for a faltering of this confidence, and for a certain receptivity to something other. But the asylum, legitimated in the languages of psychiatric and medical science and strengthened by the powerful discourse of humanism, focuses its energy on madness – the weak seam in the fabric of reason, the place where difference might break through – and welds that seam tight shut.

The point is both philosophical and political. Philosophically, there is no foundation for the claim that our system of reasonable behaviour is the definitive expression of sanity and reason in human affairs. Politically, the system of 'reason' which rules us produces such appalling consequences – military conflict, sexual and racial discriimination, starvation and exploitation, rape, murder and child molestation – that the enormous self-confidence of our reason and its representatives is conceivably nothing less than cataclysmic disaster and damnation of the human race. Against such a vision, the consoling successes of the sometimes humane treatment of lunatics, while doubtless important and heartening for those involved, is really rather small and utterly beside the point. If we live in a fractured world, then the combined efforts of science and the moralizing discourse of 'correct ideas' to prevent anyone from peering through the breaks must be treated with the greatest suspicion.

What Foucault's work on madness presents us with is an attempt to grasp a form of human existence entirely other than our own. This anthropological project is suffused by the suspicion, even at times by the belief, that vast parts of the juridical, medical and epistemological conceptualization of mental health are repressive. His text takes us back in time to uncover the complex history of mental illness. It is a history which begins with the decline of leprosy and which ends with the modern mental hospital. This story forms no part of the contemporary discourse of mental science and, since it indicts psychology, psychiatry and neurosurgery for their brutal ahistoricism, an ahistoricism which is a main precondition for the successful deployment of their major therapeutic strategies, this is not surprising. The dismissal and concealment of this history can be seen as a part of the Enlightenment project, a project which affirms that no part of the social condition is beyond analysis, and thus that the orderly workings of social power can be guaranteed through the development and application of knowledge. This project enshrines a denial of otherness, of difference. It is, effectively, *the* absolutist project, unconsciously designed along lines of complete domination. Foucault felt sure that otherness could not be left behind by the march of time. He thought that it could only be repressed. The desire that formed his words was for the return of the Other, not as fury, suffering, or a vengeful power out of control, but as the right to be different. His book was successful in exposing the economic and political roots of exclusion, and in showing the role of science in repairing the wounds inflicted by social change. As we have seen, however, the quest for otherness itself, carried through by means of an examination of art and literature, failed. Derrida will argue that this was bound to happen, that the quest for otherness cannot succeed. He will show this, not by looking to Foucault's interpretation of art, but by fastening on some apparently inconsequential remarks which Foucault made about Descartes. In order to understand the significance of these remarks, it is necessary that we familiarize ourselves with certain aspects of Descartes' philosophy, and this we will now proceed to do. In doing this, however, we should not lose sight of the very considerable significance of Foucault's text. From the beginning, his work has been a protest against the violence that is levelled against others so as to force them to become the same as us. The fact that such forced assimilation is in all probability a basic aspect of our reason, of our form of being, provides more than sufficient justification for trying to push beyond our form of reason, our form of being, in the hope that difference will be allowed to be what it is on the other side.

Notes and References.

1   Michel Foucault published *Folie et deraison: Histoire de la folie à l'âge classique* (hereafter abbreviated as HF) in 1961. A much abbreviated version was published in 1964 in a popular French paperback series. *Madness and Civilisation* (hereafter abbreviated as MC) is a translation (by Richard Howard) of the latter plus a modest amount of additional material from the original text, published in 1967. I concur with Cousins and Hussain (1984) who describe the abridged version as a 'pale version of the original'.

2   For a discussion of the problems of translating the French terms *folie* and *fou*, see Sheridan (1980), pp. 16–17. Since I shall not be concerned with fine distinctions between folly, madness, dementia, insanity, etc., I have chosen to use the generic term 'madness'. See further Felman (1975), fn. 15, pp. 224–5.

3   Michel Foucault (1977), *Discipline and Punish* (hereafter abbreviated as DP), p. 198.

4   Any exhaustive account of the history of the treatment of madness would have to begin with Hippocrates (460–375 BC), tracing the subsequent 1,300 years through to the medical institution at Salerno (ninth century AD). For a brief survey, see Neaman, Chapter 1.

5   See the important debate between Porshnev and Mousnier on the class dynamics of political power in seventeenth-century France (translated extracts of this debate will be found in Coveney [1977]). Whatever the disagreements between these two authorities, both agree that the bourgeoisie was at the centre of the political stage.

6   Ruth Pike (1982, p. 199) has shown that, in the case of Spain, it was only the poor who bore the brunt of the state's new-found idea that it 'could utilize the labour power of prisoners for its own interests'.

7   The argument that Foucault ignores the transformation of monasteries and convents into asylums (see Sedgwick [1982], p. 134) is false. Foucault discusses this very transformation in the context of his discussion of pressures against and changing attitudes within the Church with respect to the role of the monasteries and convents in the matter of poverty (see HF, pp. 68–9).

8   It is important to realize that the value of Foucault's book does not depend entirely on pinpoint historical accuracy, something that Merquior (1985, p. 27) seems to suggest when speaking of the carpet being pulled out 'from under several key assumptions in Foucault's historical picture'. Not only is it the case that Foucault's original volume is much more subtle and multi-faceted than recent critiques have suggested, it is also clear that his quest for the

meaning of confinement in relation to madness has a more than adequate historical grounding, and that it is a cultural and philosophical enterprise quite as much as a historical one.

9 Midelfort is wrong to suggest that Foucault uncritically accepts the story of Pinel's liberating the mad from their chains (Midelfort, 1980, p. 258). Even a cursory reading of the text shows that Foucault places the whole event in inverted commas, treating it as a myth (see MC, pp. 242–3), the importance of which is much less concerned with what actually happened than with its effects as presented truth.

10 MC, p. 269. There may at this point seem to be certain resemblances between the characterization advanced by Foucault and that put forward by Erving Goffman. As Hirst and Woolley (1982, pp. 183–94) have noted, however, apart from the focus on guilt which occurs in both, the political and epistemological foundations of their work are very different.

11 MC, p. 18. David Carroll (1982) speaks of this division in terms of 'high' and 'low' madness.

12 There are two paintings by Bosch titled *The Temptation of St Anthony*. The one discussed by Foucault is a triptych, housed in the National Museum of Fine Arts, Lisbon. The other, a much calmer and more contemplative study, is at the Prado, in Madrid.

13 MC, pp. 280–1. For an alternative discussion of Foucault's interpretation of Goya, see Wolin (1986).

14 The discussion of the sacred, in Descombes (1986), runs in parallel with Foucault's discussion here of the essential unknowability of madness.

15 The term 'classical' refers to the period of French history running from about 1650 to 1800.

16 See Foucault (1970), Chapter 3.

2 *The Cartesian Exclusion*

Reason was not always inscribed within a ring of indestructible confidence. Plato thought that reason emerges from the human world of shadow and illusion only with the greatest difficulty. The Judaeo-Christian tradition, founded as it is on the fundamental mysteries of God, confirms Plato's assimilation, in the allegory of the cave (Plato, 1941, Book VII) of darkness and humanity.

Descartes, however, had much more faith in the power of the human mind. Detached from the preconceptions derived from a multiplicity of sources (amongst which we might mention theology, the philosophical tradition, the common sense of everyday life passed on from one generation to the next, mysticisms of all sorts including those which posited an intimate connection between madness and wisdom, and superstitions such as those which asserted an identity between madness and witchcraft), the mind could see all the truths that there were to be seen. Not that all of them could be seen immediately, a great many of them would require the painstaking application of logic and the mechanics of cause and effect, but the core of this confidence was based in the power of the human mind to perceive basic truths clearly and distinctly. How did Descartes justify such confidence? Was he blind to the hydra-headed nature of the human condition, to madness, criminality, duplicity, lust, stupidity and greed? Was he not tempted to think that the final explanation of the place of swirling humanity within the cosmic order was beyond any rational account? If he was blind to such matters, then it was a willed blindness; for he resolved to ask only questions that he could answer, and to answer those questions only with the aid of his untrammelled mind. Freed from all preconceptions, his first subject was himself. He did not, at this point, aspire to discover some final truth about God, or about madness, or about the human condition in general. He wanted, first of all, to know what he could be certain of with respect to himself alone.

Just as Calvin thought himself to be alone before God, so Descartes sought to be alone before himself. Could such solitude produce any certainty at all? For Descartes, faith was the very condition of uncertainty that he sought to repair. So he proceeded systematically to distrust everything he would ordinarily take on trust. Only in this way could he discover if there might be some fundamental certitude about which no doubt at all would be possible. If such certainty could be achieved, then a true philosophical system might be built upon it. Such a philosophy would serve to underwrite *all* inquiry into the phenomenal world; all of the sciences could have unshakeable confidence in the solidity of their foundations.

Wherein might such certainty about himself lie? The certainty of the materiality and fleshiness of one's own body might be a place to start. Surely Descartes could not doubt the existence and solidity of his own body. But there are those who apparently do entertain such doubts. They are madmen

> whose brains are so damaged by the persistent vapours of melancholia that they firmly maintain ... that their heads are made of earthenware ... or made of glass.[1]

Descartes cannot follow their example and assume that his conception of his own body is as questionable as those who maintain themselves to be made of glass. For would he not be mad so to do? If his philosophical reflections are to be worth anything, he cannot assume himself to be mad right from the beginning.[2] Another, less extreme, but no less persuasive justification for radical doubt must be found. He will forget the deranged perceptions of those with damaged brains, and ask rather whether he might be dreaming that he had hands or legs. This is no mad thought. We have all had vivid dreams in which we seemed to be certain of our surroundings and our selves. But when we wake up we see that what we took to be real was nothing but the illusion of a dreamer.

The impossibility of providing a certain criterion for distinguishing a dream from waking reality, of *proving* that we are not dreaming *right now*, gives Descartes a justification of doubt which is much less problematic than the hypothesis of madness. Not only can he appeal to the common experience of his readers, who will all have had their dreams. He can also point to the connection between dreams and reality. Even a fantastic monster which might appear in a dream will be some sort of composite of things and characteristics that do appear in the waking world. The situation is much the same for the painter who would try to depict something entirely strange. Even if a picture is created, the like of which has never been seen before, still it is inconceivable that it will not be recognizable in the real and certain terms of colour, shape, size and quantity. Descartes' conclusions here, implicit and explicit, are threefold. First, the problem of the dream can function as 'the principal reason for doubt' (PWD II, p. 61). Second, the question of madness can be dispensed with entirely. Third, the lack of a criterion of determination as between dreaming and wakefulness does not mean that Descartes must abandon his quest for some certainty about himself, because

> whether I am awake or asleep, two and three added together are five, and a square has no more than four sides. It seems impossible that such transparent truths should incur any suspicion of being false. (PWD II, p. 14)

But, Descartes asks himself, how can I be sure that every time I add two and three to make five I do not make a mistake? Perhaps I deceive myself that a square has four sides. These are doubts so radical that even the hypothesis of the dreamer is not sufficiently extreme to confront them. A further move is needed. Perhaps Descartes thought for a time of returning to the madness hypothesis. We do not know. If he did so think, then he rejected the strategy in favour of another. Descartes posed the hypothetical suggestion that a powerful and malicious demon has him in his power, and is employing all his energies in deceiving him at every turn, even when he adds two and three and makes five. Even though hypothetically under the power of this malicious demon, Descartes will still 'resolutely guard against assenting to any falsehoods' (PWD II, p. 15). He will do everything that he can, in other words, to ensure that he is not tricked, despite being under the power of a devious and malign demon. As he points out, this will mean considering himself, for example, 'as not having hands, or eyes, or flesh, or blood' (PWD II, p. 15), but as falsely believing himself to have such things. Where now might certainty reside in such a condition?

Before answering this question, it is worth reflecting on the extreme unreasonableness of such a supposition as the malicious demon. To live in rigorous accord with this hypothesis would be madness. Yet this madness of thought is, thinks Descartes, a necessary step in the establishment of the rule of reason. Once the step has been taken, and the result achieved, this madness, so welcomingly accepted as a methodological necessity at the time, will be soon cast entirely out of mind.

Under the hypothesis of the malicious demon, Descartes has no body; there is neither earth nor sky. All that is certain is that Descartes is being deceived. Yet there is a necessary limit to the power of the deceiver. Descartes cannot be deceived into thinking that he exists if, in reality, he does not exist. It makes no sense to say that Descartes is nothing and that he is thinking. It is contradictory. So the demon can do what he will, he cannot fool Descartes on the question of his own existence. As Descartes, famously, concludes, 'Cogito ergo sum'. Here is bedrock. Descartes knows something about himself with complete certainty. He knows that as long as he is thinking, he exists. He knows himself to be, at the very least, a thinking substance. He also knows – implicitly, for he neither discusses nor admits this, and so it would perhaps be better to say believes rather than knows – that at least one law of logic is absolutely valid: the law of non-contradiction, that a thing cannot be both p and not p at the same time, that he cannot be *both* existing because thinking *and* not existing because deceived at the same time. Now that Descartes has worked all this out, he will have no more use for the hypothesis of the malicious demon. It has served its purpose and can be discarded.

Why is this belief in the law of non-contradiction not also a matter for doubt? It is because the truth of this law can be seen by the 'natural light' of the mind.[3] It is, in other words, one of the essential laws of thought itself: a *sine qua non* of reason. Otherwise could not the madman's body be both flesh and glass at the same time?

Where will Descartes proceed now that he has this fundamental certainty of his own existence in thought? Naturally enough, he would like to move from the certainty of his own existence in thought to some certainty concerning the existence of other things in the world. He knows that he is a thinking thing, and he asks:

What is that? A thing that doubts, understands, affirms, denies, is willing, is unwilling, and also imagines and has sensory perceptions. (PWD II, p. 19)

All these things he knows. Take, for example, the question of sensory perceptions. Even if he is deceived by his senses, he does know with certainty that his mind seems to perceive things in the outer world. He is also certain that *if* the things that he seems to perceive do exist, then their essential nature is grasped not by his senses, but by his mind. He shows this by considering the changes that a piece of beeswax might go through. At one moment it has taste, smell, a certain shape, temperature and hardness; but place that same piece of wax in front of a fire, and all these characteristics change. It is the same piece of wax, but all the characteristics which were formerly identified by the senses as constituting the piece of wax have changed. Thus the features which are apprehended by the senses are contingent. Take these features away, and only the mind can grasp the essence of the wax, which is that it is 'extended, flexible and changeable'. To say that the thing itself is beeswax, with all its contingent qualities, is, then, a *judgement* of the intellect, an act of reason.

To achieve the movement from his solitary thinking self to an outer reality, Descartes fastens on this question of judgement. It is in 'judging that the ideas which are in me resemble, or conform to, things located outside me' (PWD II, p. 26) that mistakes and errors may be made. Yet Descartes has to provide a warrant for at least some certain judgements. How will he do this? His answer is to invoke another of the principles of the mind's 'natural light': the principle of cause and effect.[4] He argues that the thoughts which he has must have been caused, and their cause must reside in himself or in some force outside of him. He thus concludes:

> If the objective reality of any of my ideas turns out to be so great that I am sure the same reality does not reside in me ... and hence that I myself cannot be its cause, it will necessarily follow that I am not alone in the world.[5]

He goes on to demonstrate, at least to his own satisfaction,[6] that all of his ideas, with just one exception, might be shown to have arisen in himself. Even abstract notions like number and duration could be generated by the single certainty of Descartes' existence as a thinking thing. The only idea that could not have arisen from himself is, he asserts, the idea of God. By 'God', Descartes understands 'a substance that is infinite, independent, supremely intelligent, supremely powerful' (PWD II, p. 31), and which created all that exists. This idea of God could not have originated in any human individual since, for Descartes, the effect cannot be superior to the cause. A small force cannot be the efficient cause of a much greater force; finitude and imperfection cannot efficiently produce the infinite power and perfection which God is taken to be. Joining this 'proof' (which is clearly problematic as it assumes that the mental conception of God constitutes a reality so massive that only the true God could have created it) to the notion that only an omnipotent God could re-create Descartes anew from moment to moment, Descartes concludes that 'the human intellect cannot know anything that is more evident or more certain' (PWD II, p. 37) than that God exists.

Descartes now has two certainties: that he exists as a thinking thing, and that God exists as supreme power and perfection. In addition, he has the principles of logic and cause and effect given to him by the natural light of his mind. He now proceeds to argue that God could not be a deceiver, since to practise deception is *prima facie* evidence of imperfection; but that cannot be, since God is perfection. It is important here to see that in Descartes' conception of God there is an appeal to two principles. The first is an appeal to a material principle of causality – God as a supreme power of creation. The second is an appeal to morality: the conception of perfection which Descartes attributes to God is actually a moral conception – a perfect God could not possibly be a deceiver. As we have seen in Foucault's account of the history of madness, this pairing of the material and the ethical is momentous for the modern world.

But how, then, does it arise that God created a creature who can be deceived, as when, for example, one makes a mistake in judging a distant object to be what it is actually not? Descartes, even if he does implicitly claim that the otherness of God has to stand in some relation to the ethical, does not pretend to understand all of God's purposes. He is sure, however, that error is not of the essence of the faculty of judgement. This faculty is God-given and could not have been granted with intent to deceive. Thus an error of judgement must be a defect due to human imperfection; and, what is more, it is a defect which can be avoided.

The key is in the distinction between will and intellect.[7] It is in the exercise of the will that we perhaps come closest to the combination of power and perfection that exists in God, for we can always decide in more than one way. But this power can be misused if the will is not in alignment with the intellect (or, to use another equivalent term, the understanding). Thus the avoidance of error is possible by simply exercising the will in accordance with our limited powers of understanding. We should refrain from making judgements in those cases where the intellect does 'not perceive the truth with sufficient clarity and distinctness' (PWD II, p. 41). Where we do understand clearly and distinctly, then our judgement will follow. Not that it must, but it is powerfully inclined to do so by the clarity and distinctiveness of the perception. For Descartes, when the understanding perceives something clearly and distinctly, we can be sure that it perceives truly, because God, who is not a deceiver, gave us the powers that we have, and it is inconceivable that where we perceive something clearly God intended that we should be deceived. It follows from this that corporeal things 'possess all the properties which I clearly and distinctly understand' (PWD II, p. 55).

There has been considerable debate as to whether Descartes' argument is circular: I have a clear and distinct idea of God, this idea must have been placed in me by God, the existence of God, thus proven, guarantees the truth of my clear and distinct ideas. Now, the argument about the 'Cartesian circle' has been going on for over 300 years,[8] and it would be out of place to attempt seriously to add a footnote to it here. But one aspect of it is germane to the issue of Descartes and the madness hypothesis: one way out of the circle is to posit clear and distinct ideas which are independent of God, which, in other words, do not require God's guarantee to establish their truth. These ideas are those which Descartes refers to in the terms of the 'natural light' of the mind. The laws of logic and causality are the real foundation of his argument. Without them it is almost inconceivable that even the idea of God could exist. Life and thought outside of these ideas would be absolutely Other, utter unreason. In his pursuit of certainty, Descartes has no alternative but to seal himself off from this unimaginable realm. To entertain, with any determination at all, the madness hypothesis, he would have had to enter this realm where he could not will himself to go. Thus he cannot seriously consider the possibility that God is beyond reason or arbitrary in any way. This self-imposed limitation is illustrated in the ontological argument advanced in the *Fifth Meditation* (the meditation which is most peripheral to his system as a whole, functioning only as a buttress to the *Third*), which is an attempt to provide a logical proof of the existence of a rational God. Even if the attempt succeeds, the God whose existence is so demonstrated is not a God of supreme power and infinite qualities, but a God restricted by those laws which are known to reason.

We now begin to see the significance of Descartes' thought for Foucault's exploration of madness. Descartes' pursuit of certainty proceeds by way of a double dismissal of otherness. First he rejects the hypothesis that the condition of madness might have any relevance for the rational mind. Then, he constructs God in the terms of power and morality, thereby denying the otherness of God by fashioning God as a more perfect and powerful example of himself. What exactly will Foucault make of this double avoidance and denial of difference?

Foucault and Descartes

Foucault's interpretation of Descartes occupies just three out of the 700 pages which make up *Histoire de la folie*. The interpretation appears as a kind of preface to Foucault's account of the 'great confinement', the process which began with the foundation of the General Hospital in 1656, and which was concluded with the liberation of the inmates of Bicêtre in 1794. The three pages on Descartes do not, at first glance, appear to be so important. They were not included in the abridged version of the book, or in the English translation which was based on the abridged version with some additions. What did Foucault write in them?

For Foucault, madness was allowed a voice through the medieval era and into the Renaissance. Alchemists, astrologers, magicians, prophets, miracle workers, these were figures known and credited in Renaissance life and thought. The mad fool was just one of a whole series of characters whose unreasonable existence testified to the limitations of reason. Just like the other characters, the mad had their tales to tell, and their secrets to impart. Renaissance humanism was attentive to unreason: Erasmus praised Christianity as a form of folly of greater worth than human reason; while Agrippa von Nettesheim, thought by some to have been the original model for Faust, scorned the universal pretensions of the sciences, affirmed the limitations of human reason and recognized the role of magical forces within the cosmic order. These sixteenth-century figures were by no means alone in disputing the self-sufficiency of the rational mind. Within French culture, Montaigne is the writer that quickly comes to mind, and Foucault compares him with

Descartes. The comparison is prosecuted very briefly. But it is of considerable significance. Foucault quotes only a few words from Montaigne's essay, 'That it is folly to measure truth and error by our own capacity', but the passage from which the words are taken is worth quoting at length:

> It is a stupid presumption to go about depising and condemn-
> ing as false anything that seems to us improbable; this is a
> common fault in those who think they have more intelligence
> than the crowd. I used to be like that once, and if I heard
> talk of ghosts walking, or prognostications of future events,
> of enchantments or sorceries, or some other tale that I could
> not swallow ... would pity the poor people who were taken in
> by such nonsense. And now I find that I was at least as much
> to be pitied myself; not that the experience has shown me
> anything that transcends my former beliefs, though this has
> not been for lack of curiosity; but reason has taught me that
> to condemn anything so positively as false and impossible is
> to claim that our own brains have the privilege of knowing the
> bounds and limits of God's will, and of our mother nature's
> power. I have learnt too that there is no more patent folly in
> the world than to reduce these things to the measure of our
> own power and capacity. (Montaigne, 1958, p. 87)

Montaigne's advice, then, is that anyone who would ignore unreason, who would deny otherness and difference by mak-ing themselves the measure of all things, would be guilty of unreasonableness. This is advice that Descartes cannot accept.

For Foucault, a consideration of the forms of unreason, of magic, madness, revelation, faith healing, miracles and so on, was basic to the sceptical tradition right through the sixteenth century. The Renaissance thinker is 'never certain of not being mad' (HF,[9] p. 58).

The vitality of the sceptical tradition at this time owes much to the opening of the new world; new civilizations were encoun-tered; fabulous tales found willing and credulous listeners. As Shakespeare put it, in *Hamlet*:

> There are more things in heaven and earth, Horatio,
> Than are dreamt of in your philosophy.

But Descartes must set aside the workings of excited imagina-tions. How much more difficult, for example, it would have been for Descartes to advance his 'dream' argument, if he had granted any credence to the following tale, recounted by Montaigne:

> Although there is nothing strange in seeing horns grow in the night on foreheads that had none at bedtime, there is something memorable about the case of Cippus, King of Italy. During the day he had been a passionate spectator at the bullfight, and all night long he had worn horns in his dreams. His forehead actually sprouted them by the power of the imagination. (Montaigne, 1958, pp. 37–8)

We have here a fundamental distinction between, on the one hand, the kind of thinking that will acknowledge the limits of both its actual and potential knowledge, and therefore is not prepared to dismiss unreason, and, on the other hand, the autonomy, sovereignty and sobriety of the rational subject presented by Descartes.

This distinction has a profound methodological significance. Foucault saw that Descartes was presented with three possible reasons for doubt: errors of the senses, the unreality of dreams and the illusions of the mad. The senses may lead us into error, but apparently only with respect to the things that are either very far away or very small. Dreams, like the imagination of painters, can produce fantastic things, but even the most bizarre images are constructed out of the simple and universal givens of the real world, like colour and shape. With both errors of the senses and the illusions of dreams, Foucault sees that a relation to true perception is preserved. In the former case, sense-perception misleads *only* when things are very small or far away. In the latter case, dreams may be illusory, but their nature is familiar to us from our understanding of the waking world. Thus Descartes argues *through* the cases of errors and dreams. As Foucault puts it:

> Neither the images created in sleep, nor the certain awareness that the senses can be deceived, can take doubt to the extreme point of its universality; suppose we are asleep: truth will not entirely escape into the night. (HF, p. 57)

However, Descartes treats the question of madness differently. He does not work through the madness hypothesis, emerging on its other side to stand firm on the solid ground of residual truth. Rather, he declares that he would be no less extravagant than the mad themselves if he were to follow their example and imagine that he were made of glass. Thus, instead of finding something in the thought of the mad[10] that could not be false, Descartes effectively declares that 'I who think cannot be mad' (HF, p. 57).

While it appears that the difference between Descartes' treatment of madness as against dreams and sensible error is merely that between peremptory dismissal in the former case and argument in the latter, Foucault finds that the division is much more profound. The preservation of truth in the case of dreams and sensible errors is provided for in the nature of the *object* of thought. The certainty of correctly perceiving one's immediate surroundings more than counterbalances those errors of the senses that may be made regarding distant objects; the necessary occurrence in dreams of such simple universals as shape, colour and so on, confirms that dreams are more than illusion and falsehood, and that there is the possibility of certain truth even if one is dreaming. In both of these cases, the preservation of the possibility of certain truth is achieved through an analysis of the object of thought: what the senses perceive or what the dreamer dreams. The case of madness, however, cannot be argued through because the only thing that allows the pursuit of certainty to continue with some confidence is the characterization of the *subject* who thinks as sane:

> It is not the permanence of a truth which guarantees thought against madness, as it would permit truth to detach itself from error or to emerge from a dream; it is an impossibility of being mad, essential not to the object of thought but to the subject who thinks. (HF, p. 57)

What does this philosophical exclusion of madness signify? It signifies that it is the subject who is the wellspring of truth. We are not speaking here of the subject as a body; bodies can malfunction, the brain can be invaded by dark vapours. Nor is it a question of the subject as a will. For the will is propelled by passion, and the untamed will is the source of error and sin (PWD II, p. 41). Rather, we are speaking of the subject as intellect, as thought, as the source of sovereign truth. It is this subject, the rational subject, which will become the defining figure of the post-Renaissance world. As Foucault writes:

> Between Montaigne and Descartes, something has happened; something which concerns the advent of a *logic*. But it is far from the case that a history of a logic like that of the western world is fully explained by the progress of a 'rationalism'; it derives in large part from that secret movement in which unreason is plunged deep under the ground, there no doubt to disappear, but there also to take root. (HF, p. 58)

This new logic will present itself in terms of free will and determinism or, otherwise stated, decisionistic ethics and natural science. These pairings go together. It never was a question of free will *or* determinism, but, from Descartes onward, a matter of their inseparability as the twin principles of the modern worldview.

So it is that the path of modern madness is laid out: a question of either bodily malfunction or moral fault. For as long as we live in the shadow of Cartesian dualism of autonomous mind and extended matter, it will always be a question of perceiving madness as both physical and moral failure. The essence of modern madness is to be indecidable between these two poles.

This connection between Cartesianism and modern madness is far from explicit in Foucault's interpretation of Descartes. But it is, I submit, clearly implicit in Foucault's book as a whole, proceeding, as it does, to discover both the medical and moral dimensions of the treatment of insanity.

To find this link, and then to write the history of some of its consequences, was not, however, all that Foucault had set out to do. For he wished to do that without confirming the judgement that excluded madness:

> We must speak of that initial dispute without assuming a victory, or the right to a victory; we must speak of those actions re-examined in history, leaving in abeyance all that may figure as a conclusion, as a refuge in truth; we shall have to speak of this act of scission, of this distance set, of this void instituted between reason and what is not reason, without ever relying upon the fulfillment of what it claims to be.
>
> Then, and then only, can we determine the realm in which the man of madness and the man of reason, moving apart, are not yet disjunct; and in an incipient and very crude language, antedating that of science, begin the dialogue of their breach, testifying in a fugitive way that they still speak to each other. (MC,[11] p. x)

Foucault, then, wished to escape from the form of reason that dominates, even constitutes, the modern world. He planned an odyssey towards a greater truth, as if in hope that at the end of it he would be able to say, with Descartes: 'I learned not to believe too firmly anything of which I had been persuaded only by example and custom. Thus I gradually freed myself from many errors which may obscure our natural light and make us less capable of heeding reason' (PWD I, p. 116)

At stake, then, is the possibility of a higher form of reason which would transcend the division between Western reason and its hidden other. Foucault's pursuit of the certitude that such a higher reason might bestow[12] places him in a direct line of succession from Descartes himself.

Descartes, in the *First Meditation*, was in search of absolute certainty. He used doubt as a means of discovering if such certitude might be reached. But he baulked at the prospect of doubting reason itself, and so excluded madness from thought. This exclusion is momentous. It affirms the sovereignty of the sane, rational subject with free will over an extended world of things, a world without essential quality[13] whose exploitable plasticity can be controlled by a mind which has a natural understanding of mathematical logic and causality. The consequences of this dualistic ontology have been horrific; for example, the science of nuclear weapons and germ warfare, and the decisionism of the Holocaust. Foucault does not say that such developments were due to Descartes, who is merely an expressive figure in the history of Western culture. But his work does imply that they are inherent in the project of Western reason itself. What is paradigmatic for this project is the refusal to question reason itself, and Descartes here is exemplary. But, Foucault asks, was Descartes' dismissal of madness necessary? Would it not be possible to rethink the *First Meditation*, but this time to argue through madness? Might not a different certitude emerge on its other side?

If we see Foucault's *Histoire de la folie* as a modern, but much more radical, version of the *First Meditation*, we have an explanation for a notable double absence: the lack of any discussion by Foucault of the place of God, or of the place of the malicious demon, in Descartes' system. Their absence from Foucault's account might be thought surprising. After all, both of these figures conjure up images of incomprehension in the face of the Other.

It will be recalled that Foucault saw that neither sensible error nor a lack of certainty of being awake was sufficient to push doubt to its most extreme point. In neither case does truth disappear into the night. It is because neither example forces doubt to the limit that the hypothesis of the malicious demon is advanced. But if the strategy is altered, if the possibility of madness is accepted rather than excluded, the hypothesis of the malicious demon is unnecessary. For the acceptance of the possibility of madness does take doubt to, and even beyond, its outermost point. There is no consideration of the malicious demon in Foucault's text because a serious contemplation of madness renders it strictly irrelevant. The situation with regard to the question of God is a little more complex. At one level, the absence of any discussion by Foucault of the place of God in Descartes' system can be explained in just the same way as the absence of any discussion of the malicious demon: the question of God arises subsequent to the authorization of Descartes' reason through the exclusion of madness. Since Foucault effectively re-routes the meditation before that authorization, the matter of God need not arise. But beyond this, it does seem that in general Foucault does not regard an idea of God as in any way central to the project of Western reason. Why is that?

Given the importance of Cartesianism for our form of reason, we may take Foucault as being an implicit supporter of the dissimulation thesis regarding Descartes' thought. This is the thesis that Descartes was 'not sincere in his appeal to the existence of a non-deceiving God in order to validate clear and distinct perception' (Loeb, 1986, p. 244). We have seen that it is probably necessary to affirm the validity of some ideas (specifically those concerning logic and causality) independently of any divine guarantee. Otherwise the Cartesian system appears to be circular. But, if the validity of some ideas *must* be accepted before any idea of God, and if, as is the case, the vision of God subsequently advanced is merely the apotheosis of those ideas, with God's prime attributes being the truth enshrined in logic, the power bespoken by causality, and the perfection of the moral ideal, then the idea of God becomes an adornment which is only contingently present within the system as a whole. So God can easily be subtracted from the Cartesian system, just as it can be, and many would say has been, eliminated from the project of Western reason. This subtraction, one might say, is yet another instance of arrogant reason denying the very possibility of anything beyond its power.

Foucault's project, then, was a radical one. In search of a form of being more magnanimous than our own, he sought to take himself back to that point when reason and unreason were torn asunder. He was, we have suggested, a contemporary Descartes who felt himself to be deceived. It is, however, modern reason that this time plays the role of the malign demon. A great deal is at stake in such an operation. It goes to the heart of the way that we think and the way that we are. Such accusatory disrespect for Western being could not easily be borne. No doubt it is ironic that Jacques Derrida – self-appointed scourge of Western metaphysics – should have been the first to underline the incoherence of Foucault's project. But supposing that something were to be discovered through Foucault's manoeuvres, it would hardly be the case that Foucault would then be seen as the author of a new era. His work would still be just words on the page; dumb and useless unless attuned to a parallel readiness, at the level of the general culture, to live beyond its previous history. The signs are that there is no such readiness, that otherness and difference are still prohibited.

Notes and References

1 René Descartes (1985), *Meditations on First Philosophy*, in *The Philosophical Writings of Descartes*, Vol. II, translated by John Cottingham, Robert Stoothoff and Dugald Murdoch, p. 13 (all references to this two-volume edition of Descartes' philosophical writing will hereafter be abbreviated as PWD I or PWD II).

2 Harry Frankfurt (1970, pp. 37–8) asked: 'By what right does he so airily discard the possibility that he is mad?' He went on to answer that Descartes' implicit claim that he cannot entertain the possibility of his own insanity is acceptable:

> It seems clear that he has no reasonable alternative and that it would be a mistake to regard his discussion of madness as evidence of a damaging failure to honor his commitment to doubt. The whole point of his critical examination of his former opinions is to determine whether or not there are reasonable grounds for doubting them. If he were to begin by suspending the judgement that he is reasonable, he would be unable ever to re-establish his confidence in his own ability to carry out his task. For if he were to entertain doubts about his own rationality, he would naturally be bound to suspect any reasoning by which he might attempt to establish his sanity.

3 In Descartes' system, the terms 'mind' and 'soul' are pretty much equivalent. In the first translation of *The Meditations* from the Latin into French, which appeared in 1647, we find the following gloss: 'the mind or the soul of man for I make no distinction between

them' (PWD II, p. 10). Descartes approved this translation, and very probably made minor amendments and clarifications himself. See the 'Translator's Preface', PWD II, p. 1.

4 The closest that Descartes comes, in *The Meditations*, to an explicit statement that the mind knows the principle of cause and effect by virtue of the mind's 'natural light' is the following passage from the *Sixth Meditation*:

> I must more accurately define exactly what I mean when I say that I am taught something by nature. In this context I am taking nature to be something more limited than the totality of things bestowed on me by God. For this includes many things that belong to the mind alone – for example, my perception that what is done cannot be undone, and all other things that are known by the natural light. (PWD II, p. 57)

This should be read in conjunction with Descartes' statement that 'something cannot arise from nothing' (*Third Meditation*, PWD II, p. 28). As Bernard Williams notes (1978, p. 141), Descartes thinks that everything must have a cause, and further that this 'truth' is a facet of the mind's natural light; see also Marjorie Grene's argument (1985, p. 148) that while the 'natural light' cannot understand creation, it can provide the principles of causality.

5 *Third Meditation*, PWD II, p. 29. The use of the term 'objective reality' is scholastic. The term relates to the reality inherent in ideas, and is opposed to the term 'formal reality' which pertains to the reality inherent in phenomena. See *Author's Replies to the First Set of Objections*, PWD II, pp. 74–86.

6 Perhaps the major contradiction here pertains to Descartes' idea of the material world as indefinite extension. If his argument that the mind is inferior to God and thus cannot be its cause is correct, a similar argument would suggest that Descartes' idea of the external world could not have been internally generated either; see Margaret D. Wilson (1986).

7 For a lively defence of Descartes' two-faculty theory of mind, see David M. Rosenthal (1986).

8 For a useful discussion of many aspects of this debate, see E. M. Curley (1978), Chapter 5.

9 *Folie et deraison: Histoire de la folie à l'âge classique* (abbreviated as HF throughout); see Chapter 1, fn. 1.

10 In this post-Freudian world, one might now think in terms of the discourse of the unconscious or the language of schizophrenia. But, for Foucault, while 'Psychoanalysis can unravel some of the forms of madness, it remains a stranger to the sovereign enterprise of unreason' (MC [see fn. 11], p. 278).

11 *Madness and Civilisation* (abbreviated as MC throughout); see Chapter 1, fn. 1.

12 In the course of a personal, unrecorded conversation with me in 1978, Michel Foucault did reluctantly admit that his book on madness might be seen as a quest for certitude.

13   'Descartes intuitively knows his first principles, the simple natures,
     thought and existence. They determine ontologically what there is,
     because the truth of clear and distinct perception is unproblematic.
     The Cartesian foundational problem is not to defend the immu-
     tability of these principles against a doubt that could never be
     defeated if it were successfully raised, but rather the need to
     secure access to a world wholly divested of quality – it is
     the methodological problem of outwitting [the] prejudice that
     conceals the world' (Caton, 1973, pp. 157–8).

3 Derrida and Foucault

Foucault's *Histoire de la folie* presents the thesis that neither scientific nor moral conceptions of mental illness can be adequately understood except in relation to the establishment of secular reason as supreme arbiter of the natural order. It was the establishment of a godlike subjective reason which resulted in the transformation of madness from an ontological to a physical-moral condition, and which denied its existence as transgression or even as humble difference. Foucault speaks, metaphorically, of this coming of reason as the Decision. He thinks of it as an extended event which took place in the seventeenth century. He saw that the advent of this reason required, as a matter of logical and political necessity, the exclusion and delegitimation of all those forms of thinking, acting and being which did not harmonize with this new despotic rationality. Some aspects of the absolute intolerance of reason to any opposition are still clearly with us today, and are found in the oppositions which many of us take for granted. Amongst these utterly confident oppositions, we might mention those between right and wrong, true and false, normal and pathological, sane and insane. What Foucault cannot speak of, however, are those unstable configurations which might emerge from outside our frameworks of thought. If such *other* configurations actually once had a place alongside those forms of being which are more familiar to us, they have been banished and we can hardly even guess at what they were.

In showing how the absolute status of the oppositions that structure modern reason is contingent upon a certain, well-concealed history, Foucault implies that things, given different historical antecedents, could have been otherwise. His book on madness is haunted by this 'otherwise', by this alternative condemned to silence by history.

Foucault aspired to break this silence and speak the language of difference. This will to transgress, present, as Derrida remarked,[1] in the *pathos* of his book, explains much of the appeal of Foucault's work for radical thinkers. His early work may be seen as an attack upon Marxism.[2] His later work, as we will see, seems to indicate the dissipation of his belief in the possibility of inaugurating a different form of reason. The proliferation of persuasive interpretations such as these, however, has not disqualified his work from receiving a great deal of attention from those who are critical of modern society. A major reason for this has been that in spite of the emergence of a pessimistic cast to his thought, Foucault's re-readings of history at least focused attention, in new and often surprising ways, on the marginal groupings in Western society. If his writings, subsequent to the madness book, seem less optimistic, even more negative than was previously the case, a determined interest in the processes of social exclusion remained central.

In *Histoire de la folie*, however, Foucault could not yet be seen as a premier representative of philosophical pessimism. Derrida's attack, about which we might speak of the action of reason defending itself, was one of the main forces which pushed him in that direction.

Derrida's commentary has a double strategy. First, he will show that, from classical Greece to the contemporary world, there is only one form of reason. So whatever occurred in the seventeenth century could not have been the advent of reason with its concomitant exclusion of unreason. Second, he will show that Foucault's reading of Descartes is wrong, and that madness is not excluded from his thought and can therefore be (as Foucault achingly thought it could not) an object of philosophical reflection. Should this double critique triumph, then Foucault's appeal to otherness will be denied by the high court of reason. This appeal to the possibility of an ungrounded future, to what Foucault called 'a truth without recourse',[3] perhaps to an end to power, will be summarily denied. Foucault will accept that judgement. Such a direct appeal will never appear from his pen again. His irrational, even mad, desire for a different kind of social order, and for a different relation between ideas and reality, will have disappeared from view.

The tactics of reason should be attended to. For there are lessons to be learnt from their success in dismissing the possibility that such an alternative could even be thought. Against our form of reason, it might even be said that such an alternative must be thought: why should our dreams be only nightmares of global conflict fuelled by xenophobia and resolved only by the obliteration of difference?

The Critique

In 1963, Derrida read a paper on the subject of Michel Foucault's *Histoire de la folie*. The lecture was subsequently published in a form which was faithful to the oral presentation. Derrida's argument has a double structure. It questions the general logic of Foucault's concept of reason, and it challenges Foucault's interpretation of Descartes in a quite specific fashion.

Let me begin with the attempted invalidation of Foucault's concept of reason. Foucault wrote:

> In the serene world of mental illness, modern man no longer communicates with the madman: on the one hand, the man of reason delegates the physician to madness, thereby authorising a relation only through the abstract universality of disease; on the other, the man of madness communicates with society only by the intermediary of an equally abstract reason which is order, physical and moral constraint, the anonymous pressure of the group, the requirements of conformity. As for a common language, there is no such thing; or, rather, there is no such thing any longer; the constitution of madness as a mental illness, at the end of the eighteenth century, affords the evidence of a broken dialogue, posits the separation as already effected, and thrusts into oblivion all those who stammered imperfect words without fixed syntax in which the exchange between reason and madness was made. The language of psychiatry, which is a monologue of reason *about* madness, has been established only on the basis of such a silence. I have not tried to write the history of that language, but rather the archaeology of that silence. (MC,[4] pp. x–xi)

This is one of several formulations that occur in the original preface to the book. They attest to Foucault's desire to go beyond our reason, the reason of the Western world to which one might, he suggests at one point without following the thought through, contrast the mysteries of the Orient (HF [1961], p. iv). They attest to his desire somehow to confront the experience of madness itself:

> it is definitely not a question of a history of ideas, but of the rudimentary movements of an experience. A history not of psychiatry, but of madness itself, in its vivacity, before

knowledge has even begun to close in on it. (HF [1961], p. vii)

Foucault did not want to write about psychiatry; he wanted to touch madness itself.

We can see two projects here: first to know madness in its primitive, untamed state; and secondly to give an account of the historical necessities underlying the exclusion of the mad and the silencing of madness. Both projects will seek to avoid complicity with the forces of repression and domination which excommunicated madness by fabricating its 'truth'.

Derrida asserts that Foucault's desire that madness be the *'subject* of his book in every sense of the word' is the maddest aspect of the work. For Derrida there is a simple trap, which is to think that one can reach out and into madness by the use of the very instrument that had previously banished it, that instrument being the language of reason. Derrida believes Foucault to be well aware of this difficulty, but he argues that Foucault's determination to circumvent the difficulty produces an unsatisfactory plurality of approaches: at one instant, madness is associated with silence, the next instant, it is a question of a language that speaks by and to itself, and the next instant after that, madness appears to be assimilated to a kind of pure negativity. For Derrida, there are fundamental problems with each of these attempts to formulate a conceptual path through to madness itself.

Consider, first, the question of madness and silence. The silence of madness is brimful with meaning! How do we know that this absence of communication is so significant? We can know this only if the significance is somehow communicated to us. It must, in some way, be documented. The silence must be signified in such a way that we can read its significance. But what could be the language of such signs? Would it not have to be the language of reason? Would not such signs tell us that there is nothing in madness other than malfunction? As Foucault defines it, reason could say nothing else to us about madness. If aspiring to go beyond that reason, one could only conclude that reason is false, that it is performing the function of prohibition. As Derrida puts it, 'all these signs and documents are borrowed, without exception, from the juridical province of interdiction' (CHM, p. 35). But if reason is false here, how are we to rely on the language of the signs that tell us of the silence of madness? Such contradictions are not easy to overcome. Derrida's argument does not need to be comprehensive. He does not consider a sample of these 'documents' used by Foucault so as to show that they are all irreparably compromised by reason. He does not consider the deployment of artworks in Foucault's text, nor the functioning of literary works.[5] Derrida thinks (silently) to himself that such pedestrian demonstrations are not necessary, for all he needs to show is that such 'signs and documents' *by definition* communicate meanings, and hence are *in their meaningfulness* a part of reason. Thus, the path to a knowledge of madness, which would take us to madness along the road indicated by its silence, must remain in the thrall of the reason which forbids the very existence of its other.

As for a language that would speak only to itself, Derrida has nothing to say. But it would hardly be necessary for him to explain Wittgenstein's arguments against the idea of a private language simply in order to point out that if a language spoke only to itself then *we* could never understand it.

Can madness then be considered as pure negativity? Derrida does not answer this question even though he raises it. This is, at first sight, surprising, in view of the place of the concept of nothingness in modern French philosophy.[6] But, after further thought, the reason that Derrida does not pursue the matter is plain enough. For Derrida the idea of negativity does not refer to some transcendental reality, but is rather an effect of language. Since language is the medium of reason, the notion of negativity cannot convey us to the secret heart of madness. Such a vehicle is one from which it would never be possible to alight.

In sum, neither silence, nor a perfectly secret language, nor pure negativity, will help Foucault; these are not ideas that can convey him to madness itself. 'But', says Derrida, 'everything transpires as if Foucault *knew* what madness means' (CHM, p. 41). He does not, however, conclude that Foucault's enterprise is fraudulent, but rather concludes, with Foucault, that the essence of madness is that it cannot be said:

> To say madness without expelling it into objectivity is to let it say itself. But madness is by essence what cannot be said; it is the 'absence of the work' as Foucault profoundly says.[7]

Thus the experience of madness is not *in* the book. It is registered only by a certain depth of feeling, a pathos, a longing for madness that simultaneously desires satisfaction and embraces the frustration guaranteed by the fact that language is reason's tool.

Nevertheless, even if madness cannot be reached by reason, perhaps its story can be written. This story would provide an account of the forces that combined to produce this impenetrable zone. It would be, to use Foucault's phrase, an archaeology of silence. And, although the suggestion is made neither by Foucault nor Derrida, perhaps such an archaeology would be more than an archaeology of *this* silence; perhaps it can be a model for archaeologies of other silences, of other exclusions. There is promise in such a strategy, even a degree of the Enlightenment spirit.

Derrida rejects the possibility of an 'archaeology of silence'. There is a strong argument which accompanies this rejection. But there is also the question of why that argument was deployed. If, metaphorically speaking, Derrida *is* reason, there was no choice about the matter. In Cartesian language, the clear and distinct idea will be decisive, and the argument has to be advanced. Let us consider the argument first of all. Derrida writes:

> is there a history of silence? Further, is not an archaeology, even of silence, a logic, that is an organised language, a project, an order, a sentence, a syntax, a work? Would not the archaeology of silence be the most efficacious and subtle restoration, the *repetition*, in the most irreducibly ambiguous meaning of the word, of the act perpetrated against madness – and be so at the very moment when this act is denounced. (CHM, p. 35)

We should not mince words; Derrida accuses Foucault of hypocrisy. He states, plainly enough, that the archaeologist of madness is in bad faith:

> All our European languages, the language of everything that has participated, from near or far, in the adventure of Western reason – all this is the immense dclegation of the project defined by Foucault under the rubric of the capture or objectification of madness. *Nothing* within this language, and *no one* among those who speak it can escape the historical guilt – if there is such, and if it is historical in the classical sense – which Foucault apparently wishes to put on trial. But such a trial may be impossible, for by the simple fact of

their articulation the proceedings and the verdict unceasingly reiterate the crime. (CHM, p. 35)

How good is Derrida's argument? Let us try to think through a case which may in certain respects be parallel. Many think that it is outrageous for white South Africans to claim that they know what is best for the indigenous Black population. What seems to be involved in the South African case is a denial of basic human freedoms. The Black population would speak for themselves if they were allowed to. They cannot easily do so because they are oppressed. One can go further and note that an anthropologist studying a Bantu village in the spirit of objective science, with utter disregard for the political and economic condition of the people being studied, could be seen as lacking in humanity to an almost criminal extent. These situations may not seem strictly comparable, because the mad, by definition (if the definition is right) cannot speak to us, by definition cannot speak for themselves. But, if *our* reason silenced and sanitized madness, might this not parallel the way in which *our* economy and *our* ethnocentrism created South African oppression? In both cases the answer would seem to be clear: for madness, we should search out a form of reason that does not exclude; for an end to oppression, we should search out forms of economy and structures of attitudes that are not dehumanizing. We may have no guarantees of success, but the commitment to the search should avoid the hypocrisy of which Derrida murmurs. If there can be not the slightest possibility, in any possible world, of an alternative reason, of an alternative economics, of an alternative structure of attitudes, then, perhaps, silence would be the only response that avoided repetition of the original sin. But the commitment to alternatives is precisely what characterizes those who are seriously concerned about all forms of social repression. It is a commitment which informs Foucault's book.

But such a commitment is, for Derrida, quite hopeless in the case of reason. As we will see, Derrida can and will commit himself to alternatives in the case of a historically contingent state of affairs such as South Africa. He cannot concede, however, that there exists a higher form of reason than the one we know. As far as he is concerned, to disengage oneself from the discursive order which has already achieved the banishment of unreason, there is only one strategy, to become mad. He is sure that whoever wishes to speak of madness and its silence, or somehow to speak within that silence, has already passed to the side of the enemy, to the side of order and rationality. For Derrida, the only spokespeople for the mad are those who betray them. He is sure of this because, for him, the condition of reason is not that of a contingent order or a structure of fact. It is not an historically determined structure which could be otherwise. Therefore, any attempt to work against reason will always be contained by reason; reason-in-general cannot be exceeded.

As I hope to have suggested by briefly discussing the case of South Africa, there is something disturbing about Derrida's argument. It would not be fair to suggest that it is tinged with a certain spirit of collaboration. To suggest that would not be fair because the collaboration of which we would be talking would be a collaboration that Derrida thinks no sentient and communicating human being could avoid. He will not deny that the works of reason are far from universally praiseworthy, but he can think of no alternative. His reason assures him that reason-in-general cannot be surpassed. He can only know this because he is in reason's power:

> The unsurpassable, unique and imperial grandeur of the order of reason, that which makes it not just another actual order or structure (a determined historical structure, one structure among other possible ones), is that one cannot speak out against it except by being for it, that one can protest it only from within; and within its domain. Reason leaves us only the recourse to stratagems and strategies. (CHM, p. 36)

Derrida's position here is different from Foucault's. We have suggested that Foucault, rather like a latter-day Descartes, distrusts our reason. His confrontation with it is reminiscent of Descartes' intellectual struggle with the 'evil genius'. Derrida's position is rather different. It is virtually identical to that of Madame Dubois in de Sade's *Justine* who, if forced to recognize the validity of God (as Derrida is forced to accept the unsurpassability of reason) would find compensation 'in perpetually irritating whatever I found that bore his impress or bespoke his touch' (de Sade, 1966, p. 714). Such strategies of irritation in the face of the unsurpassable are not yet enough for Foucault; although they will become so as his mind turns, from 1970 onwards, to the inescapability of power. The Foucault of the madness book, however, has not yet abandoned the possibility of a form of reason beyond our own. He is less confident than Derrida, because he does not believe that he knows it already, and because of his secret fear that all forms of reason will necessarily be tied to exclusion.

Histoire de la folie is written as an intrepid confrontation with this fear: it is an attempt to formulate a non-exclusionist discourse. The obstacles are formidable, and chief among them is the self-destructive thought that the machinery of exclusion is being used to search out a place from which no one will be exiled. Derrida avers that Foucault *knows* the impossibility of his project; but, unlike Derrida, Foucault was not certain of failure. He feared it – perhaps too much – but he did not resign himself to it. That the language of exclusion, that is to say the language of reason, is to be used to combat exclusion is not necessarily perverse: force can be used for good or ill, fire to warm or destroy. The existence of an ethics and a secret Utopianism in Foucault's project should not be the sole and decisive ground of criticism.

Foucault gave us a clue as to what a non-exclusionist reason might be like. He remarked that Greek reason had no contrary. This was not a statement backed up by unimpeachable scholarship. It appears to be a mere aside. But Derrida saw it as more than that, and was right to think so. However, instead of seeing the function of this apparently casual statement as a support to a certain optimism, as referring to the possibility that here might be some sort of model for a society which allowed difference to be itself, Derrida saw it only as a mistake. This is the passage from Foucault where the 'mistake' appears:

> The Greeks had a relation to something that they called *hubris*. This relation was not merely one of condemnation; the existence of Thrasymachus or of Callicles suffices to prove it, even if their language has reached us already enveloped in the reassuring dialectic of Socrates. But the Greek Logos had no contrary. (MC, p. xi)

Hubris is a word meaning contempt, insolence, or outrage. Foucault's use of the word in association with the figures of Callicles and Thrasymachus indicates that what is at issue here is an opposition to reason in the name of power and egoism. What Socrates did in Plato's *Gorgias* and *The Republic*, through reasonable argument, was to show the internal inconsistencies of a personal philosophy based on the abuse of power. He did not exclude his opposition from debate, the point being that the very dissension between Socratic reason and its other was traced out in dialogue. He did not argue against power or personal interest as such, but folded these notions into a wider and more reasonable context. Foucault is saying that even though Socrates' intent may somewhat distort the force of the position advanced by Callicles and Thrasymachus – we hear their words as reported by Plato, after all – nevertheless, we can still recognize their ambition, which is to deploy reason in their own favour, to present themselves as reasonable. Their attempts to present themselves as reasonable, in confrontation with Socrates, may fail; but Foucault's point is that, even so, reasonableness was the measure. How else would the place of rhetoric and sophistry be so central in Greek public life? Whatever the statement, intention, or action, it would be measured, by the Greeks, in the light of reason. This is what Foucault meant when he wrote that the reason of the Greeks had no contrary; and the reassuring aspect of the Socratic dialectic is presented by his demonstration that as long as reason is the measure of all things then wisdom will triumph. The outcome of this is that Greek reason, *in so far as it did not exclude its would-be usurpers*, differs from what we now take to be reason *tout court*.

Derrida did not read Foucault's statement in this way. He argues that if the Socratic dialectic is reassuring this can only be because whatever it is that reason cannot face has already been exiled. Had this not happened, then the Socratic dialectic could not be reassuring; and if it had happened, then the momentous exclusion located by Foucault in the seventeenth century 'could not have been born with classical reason' (CHM, p. 40). Derrida concludes:

> Foucault cannot *simultaneously* save the affirmation of a reassuring dialectic of Socrates and his postulation of a specifity of a classical age whose reason would reassure itself by excluding its contrary, that is, by *constituting* its contrary as an object in order to be protected from it and be rid of it. In order to lock it up. (CHM, p. 40)

But Derrida's argument is plainly one-sided. He can only see the confidence of reason as based on exclusion. Such a view is pleasing for him; since he also knows that this exclusion will be the mythical origin of the philosophical tradition. Thus his argument against Foucault does two things: it legitimates the whole history of philosophy as the story of reason (and could there be any more important site for analysis and reinterpretation?), and it enables Derrida to locate himself at a critical angle to this history, since he can argue that it is founded on a myth of origins: as he writes,

> The attempt to write the history of the decision, division, difference runs the risk of construing the division as an event or a structure subsequent to the unity of an original presence. (CHM, p. 40)

This is crucial since, as we shall see in the next chapter, the very core of Derrida's philosophy is a critique of presence.

For Derrida, the division between reason and unreason did not occur with the birth of classical reason in the seventeenth century, nor at the time of Socrates, nor with the pre-Socratics (although he notes that the fascination which the pre-Socratics exercised over Heidegger and Nietzsche, for example, may be explained by the possibility that the division is located there). The division is precisely mythical, and what Foucault has done, he implies, is to present a modern version of an immemorial myth. Derrida's argument, however, depends on his belief that the effectiveness and confidence of reason is tied to the exclusion of unreason, an exclusion which is always already achieved. It is, as I have said, Foucault's hope that reason can exceed such self-limitation; if Greek reason could confidently embrace whatever challenged it or opposed it, perhaps the way ahead is not so dark.[8] Unfortunately, there is another side to this story of reason and exclusion that was not really touched by either Foucault or Derrida. This concerns what actually happened to Athenian philosophy in the very context of the Platonic era. The fact is that there was a reaction against reason. In debating with its opponents, and in re-educating through dialogue rather than annihilating through exclusion, reason perhaps even sought to rationalize the irrational. Whether this might be seen as the subtlest form of exclusion imaginable does not matter, for the forces of opposition were mobilized against what Socrates represented. It was made a crime to disbelieve in the supernatural. It became an offence to practise or teach astronomy. Dodds recounts what happened in the years leading up to the close of the fourth century BC:

> a series of heresy trials which is unique in Athenian history. The victims included most of the leaders of progressive

thought at Athens – Anaxagoras, Diagoras, almost certainly
Protagoras also, and possibly Euripides. In all these cases
save the last the prosecution was successful: Anaxagoras
may have been fined and banished; Diagoras escaped by
flight; so, probably, did Protagoras; Socrates, who could
have done the same, or could have asked for a sentence of
banishment, chose to stay and drink the hemlock. All these
were famous people. How many obscurer persons may have
suffered for their opinions we do not know. But the evidence
we have is more than enough to prove that the Great Age of
Greek Enlightenment was also, like our own time, an Age of
Persecution – banishment of schoiars, blinkering of thought,
and even (if we can believe the tradition about Protagoras)
burning of books. (Dodds, 1968, p. 189)

What is one to conclude from this? It is very tempting to say,
with Derrida, that reason can only be constituted through
exclusion. Is it not to play a supremely dangerous game even
to countenance the weakening of reason that might be the
consequence of opening dialogue with forces of opposition?
Can we risk the return of the repressed? Foucault may have
been optimistic, but was not his Utopianism also foolish?

There is no doubt that such disputes over the nature of reason
may seem strange, even incomprehensible, to minds accustomed
to rather more tangible matters, to debates over ends and values,
and to resolvable questions of how particular ends may first be
agreed and then achieved. Foucault's quest is to find out how
this particular structure came to be *our* form of reason, and
what the consequences of this form of reason are. For those
who cannot imagine that things could be otherwise, perhaps
this quest makes no sense; there are plenty of philosophical
objections to it, most of them turning on the impossibility
of thinking outside our own framework of thought. Foucault
was aware of the difficulties, although he did not see himself
irrevocably bound by what Derrida calls the Hegelian law, that
'the revolution against reason can only be made within it'.[9]

In order to begin addressing these difficulties of going beyond
our form of reason, Foucault resorted to a certain historicism,[10]
to the view that reason has had different forms at different times
in history. Derrida describes the project that results from such
a historicizing strategy as 'an archaeology of reason', and in his
view such a project is even more ambitious than the archaeology
of silence. For Derrida, archaeology is just another name for

history and, since the historian's work is ordered and rational, history itself is an efflux of reason; reason is the condition and possibility of history. How, then, could there be a history of the conditions of possibility of history? Faced with 'the fundamental permanence of the logic-philosophical heritage' (CHM, p. 39), Derrida cannot see how an archaeology of reason is possible. The proper way to proceed, he suggests, would be to begin from the necessary assumption that *both* classical reason and classical madness are determined by reason–in–general (CHM, p. 37):

> If there is a historicity proper to reason in general ... [it] must be that of one of its determined figures. (CHM, p. 43)

And so we are back to the history of madness, not to the archaeology of silence, which Derrida thought himself to have proved an impossible project, but to the history of reason's changing accounts of madness.

In the argument detailed above, Derrida clearly commits himself to the view that there cannot be a history against reason. Is this view correct? Derrida's *a priorism* excuses him from the task of interrogating Foucault's notion of archaeology, for it will only be another form of rational inquiry hiding under a new name. We need to look a little deeper into the notion of archaeology to see if Derrida's confidence is justified.

Contrary to Henning's (1982, p. 180) view that while Foucault's '*Archaeology* contains certain criticisms of earlier works ... nowhere does it repudiate *Madness and Civilisation*', *The Archaeology*, published by Foucault some eight years after *Histoire de la folie*, is decisively different from that earlier work. Not only does Foucault say, across that space of nearly a decade, that the latter work accorded far too great and enigmatic a place to the experimental quest for an anonymous and general subject of history;[11] he also proclaimed, with hardly any reservation, opposition to 'the search for an original foundation that would make rationality the *telos* of humankind' (AK, p. 13). There is thus little doubt, and this is something that most commentators are agreed upon (see, for example, Lentricchia, 1980, p. 192), that by 1969 Foucault had abandoned any attempt to find a higher reason above our own. We will consider, a little later, why this change took place (and take place it did, contrary to some views of Foucault's work which see only continuity between the madness book and the later work, in terms of the analysis of power),[12] but, in the mean time, it should be clear that we cannot dig deeper into Foucault's idea of archaeology, as it existed in 1961, by simply turning to his work in 1969. We must rather see what archaeology meant in *Histoire de la folie*. Was Derrida right to dismiss it as just history by another name?

Since there is no discussion of the concept of archaeology in *Histoire de la folie*, and since the later elaboration of archaeology challenges some of that book's guiding assumptions, we seem to be left only with the general meaning of the term. The archaeologist finds traces of the past in the present. These remnants were left by those who are no longer with us, but the archaeologist assumes that it is possible to make some sense of them. The principles which underlie this work of 'making sense' are derived from the experience of the present. Thus the reconstruction of Roman household routines, based on the presence of foundations and various artefacts found at a particular site, will be couched in terms of certain cultural generalities like cooking, cleaning, washing, sleeping, entertaining visitors and, in general, the division of labour in the household with respect to these activities. If something is found that cannot be understood, the archaeologist sets it to one side and waits in hope that a key will be discovered; this was the case, for example, with Egyptian hieroglyphics, which were partly incomprehensible until the discovery and decoding of the Rosetta Stone.

On the basis of this brief characterization of archaeology, we can see two important features. First, an implicit belief in continuity, a belief which underpins the *a priori* assumption of the intelligibility of the past; and second, a readiness to wait and see if something will be dug up which will throw light on things discovered but not yet understood. These associated features by no means sharply distinguish archaeology from history. Indeed it is perfectly possible to understand the study of history in this way. In this case, then, Derrida was probably right to regard archaeology as pretty much equivalent to history. But the principles of continuity, intelligibility and discovery describe the kind of enterprise which Foucault was engaged upon in a more illuminating way than does a characterization of it as mere history. There was a point to Foucault's use of the term 'archaeology', a point which has been lost by Foucault's *later* counter-characterization of archaeology in terms of discontinuity and the denial of supra-historical essences. The point was that Foucault hoped to fold madness and unreason back into history. The book was, as he later said, an experiment.

He hoped to discover continuity where seemingly it could not be found. It was the failure of the experiment, and Derrida's powerful deployment of reason to show that such failure was inevitable, that brought it about that Foucault would be taken as emphasizing the discontinuities, rather than the underlying search for continuity, in the history of madness. And so it is that the commentators now automatically associate Foucault's archaeology with the surface effects of disruption and discontinuity, surface effects whose existence is, we are told, not to be explained in the terms of some underlying essence.[13] It should be noted, however, that there is a certain functional equivalence between Foucault's quest for a higher reason, in *Histoire de la folie*, and the later assertion of the principle of discontinuity, to be found in *The Order of Things* and *The Archaeology*. Both principles, even though superficially so different, attest to the possibility that the order of the world is not fixed as it is. Persuaded that the recovery of a higher reason was founded on a myth of origins, Foucault nevertheless did not have to abandon his resistance. For internal to the principle of discontinuity is the thought of absolute difference: the same thought that had inspired the work on madness. As we have seen, however, Derrida will not allow this either, because for him there is only *one* reason. Under the influence of such a belief, all that is left are strategies of irritation and annoyance. Global resistance becomes utter complicity.[14]

What all this amounts to is that Derrida sought to show that there can be no privileged space outside of reason, no higher reason, no other reason, no unreasonable reason outside of the confines of reason itself. To think of escape is impossible. Thus, in so far as he will go along with Foucault's hypothesis of the exclusion of madness, it will be a matter of internal exile. He suggests the term dissension to refer to this moment of internal cleavage:

> The issue is therefore to reach the point at which the dialogue was broken off, dividing itself between two soliloquies – what Foucault calls, using a very strong word, the *Decision* ... I would prefer *dissension*, to underline that in question is a self-dividing action, a cleavage and torment interior to meaning *in general*, interior to logos in general. (CHM, p. 38)

If madness is subject only to internal exile, perhaps, Derrida suggests, Foucault has overstated the antipathy between reason and madness. Derrida will expand upon this by challenging Foucault's interpretation of the Cartesian exclusion. He will show that Descartes did deal with madness *inside thought*.

This demonstration will harmonize with Derrida's philosophical outlook, which is that the reality behind concepts cannot be reached, that the point of arrival at this reality will always be deferred by the creation of another concept. In this respect, the idea of madness has no privilege over, say, the idea of truth. In neither case can the essence behind the idea be reached. Derrida believes Foucault to have been in error in the same way that the Western philosophical tradition as a whole has been in error. The error consists of the belief that there is something present behind the concept, and that whatever does lie behind the concept (or behind the sign, or the word) can be reached. However, there is nothing which will show madness to escape the necessary relation between reason and absence.

This general critique of the 'metaphysics of presence', which we will discuss in more detail in the next chapter, is developed in Derrida's work over the 1960s and 1970s. But we can see it in outline in both his general critique of Foucault's project and in his specific rebuttal of Foucault's interpretation of Descartes. It is to the latter that we now turn.

Derrida prefaces his examination of the *First Meditation* with yet another general point against Foucault. He argues that Foucault never really explains the historical status of the Cartesian exclusion (or of internment itself). Derrida thinks that Foucault deals with this exclusion as a kind of symptom, as, in other words, the discursive efflorescence of a structural totality. This gives rise to two questions. First, can questions of historical causation be dismissed; can we be satisfied with an incurious presentation of Descartes' text that does not squarely address its causal antecedents and its historical consequences? Second, has Foucault understood the Cartesian text correctly, at the level of 'the internal and autonomous analysis of the philosophical content of philosophical discourse' (CHM, p. 44)? The justice of Derrida's questioning pertains to the truth that Foucault does not make his philosophy of history explicit, and this is particularly clear so far as the presentation of Descartes is concerned. There is, however, an injustice in Derrida's suggestion that the status of internment is unclear: this is a remarkably insensitive remark, given that one of Foucault's main achievements is precisely to render problematic the status of internment. In fact, what lies behind Derrida's call for philosophical rigour is a certain displeasure at Foucault's marginalization of philosophy. This displeasure is evidenced both by the reference to philosophical autonomy, rooted, presumably, in the oneness of reason, and, as we will now see, by the very structure of Derrida's interpretation of the *First Meditation*, which opposes the depth of the philosopher's understanding to the naïvety of the ordinary citizen.

Derrida's counter-interpretation of Descartes denies that the three stages of Cartesian doubt (suspicion of sense-impressions, the possibility of everything being a dream, the hypothesis of the malign demon) are consecutive, with each stage being more radical than the previous one, and madness being dismissed at the outset as a possibility that must be excluded by the very nature of the enterprise. Rather, Derrida understands the *First Meditation* to be a dialogue between Descartes as philosopher and a hypothetical discussant representing the common sense of ordinary life. Specifically, Descartes' philosophy lesson begins with his intention to doubt whatever can be doubted. He demonstrates that the senses can mislead, and suggests therefore that all sensory impressions must be open to doubt. The imaginary non-philosopher finds this too extreme, and says that there are surely some things that cannot be doubted, such things as the fact that here we are sitting in front of the fire, with a pen in our hand, and a piece of paper at the ready. Furthermore, if anyone were to doubt such things, thinking themselves to be made of glass, for example, when obviously they are not, they would be mad, and one would have to be mad to follow their example. This, let it be noted, is the peasant's objection – we will come back to this. At this point, Descartes has a problem. He has to persuade his naïve companion that even such things as the apparent certainty of our immediate surroundings can be doubted. So, with a word of reassurance (a sop to stupidity, one might even say), confirming that both he and his companion are sane, a duplicitous confirmation in Derrida's view, Descartes asserts that they might be dreaming. It is only apparently the case that the dream hypothesis is less radical than the supposition of madness. For Derrida, the possibility that we might be dreaming *now* is actually more insane than mere madness; mad people, after all, are generally lucid about some things. The dialogue between philosopher and non-philosopher concludes with the former persuading the latter that even if they are dreaming there are still some things that remain certain, the basic principles of arithmetic and geometry, for instance. At this point, the philosopher dismisses the peasant, and begins his philosophical work proper. There are still some apparent certainties, and to dismiss them neither the hypothesis of madness nor what Derrida calls the 'natural hyperbole' of the dream *is mad enough*. So Descartes conceives the *total madness* of the malign demon: he will suppose himself falsely to believe that there is a sun in the sky and that he is made of flesh and blood, even that two and two make four. This, thinks Derrida, is the absolute otherness of madness which Foucault desired to know: 'a madness which will bring subversion to pure thought' (CHM, p. 53). Thus we come to the point of Derrida's reading of Descartes: even embracing the hypothesis of total madness represented by the malign demon, Descartes still came to the certainty of 'Cogito ergo sum'. That he found this place to stand, unshakeable, even from within the condition of total madness, confirms not that reason must exclude madness as a condition of its supremacy, but that the circumvention of madness is not needed at all. Derrida draws his conclusion, a conclusion entirely opposite to Foucault's:

> Madness is therefore, in every sense of the word, only one case of thought (*within* thought). (CHM, p. 56)

The last five pages of Derrida's lecture present, in the most difficult language, an explanation of what his critique is about. He does not wish to say that there is no madness. He is also prepared to acknowledge that a certain madness may be our form of unreason. What he objects to is Foucault's argument that a whole history of reason began in the seventeenth century. This, thinks Derrida, is a fundamental mistake which leads Foucault to speak of madness as if it were the same as the absolutely unspeakable other of reason-in-general, and as if its exclusion were a precondition for meaning and historicity. But whatever the nature of that precondition might be, and we can never know it, both madness and reason are subsequent to it. Both reason and unreason can have a history, and Derrida thanks Foucault for teaching him that their histories share a common tempo that is somehow made possible by the mythical origin of a long ago that is outside time. For Derrida, *our* unreason is precisely the other side of *our* reason, and both sides of our reason subsist in the atmosphere of meaning and historicity. What Derrida seems to say is that it is permissible to write some kind of history of unreason, but that it is not permissible to question reason-in-general. Madness itself does not do this, nor should Foucault. His lecture is a defence of philosophy, a brilliant apology which establishes that to the extent that histories of unreason are possible, far from throwing the world of philosophy into a turmoil, they legitimize philosophy as the history of the other side of madness:

> what Michel Foucault teaches us to think is that there are crises of reason in strange complicity with what the world calls crises of madness. (CHM, p. 63)

It is an interesting thought, Derrida seems to say, that the long calendar on which are marked the crises of confidence that have afflicted reason from the pre-Socratics through to the present day may be flipped over, and we might find corresponding undulations on the calendar of unreason.

This is an unexpected response to a work about unreason which seemed to declare the marginality of the philosophical tradition. But what it does is to re-establish philosophy as the controlling form of thought across both reason and its others, no matter in what guise these others may appear.

Foucault's Replies

Foucault made no unified response to Derrida's critique. Five years after its written publication, Foucault replied direct to Derrida, in a paper entitled 'My body, this paper, this fire'. But this reply was concerned only implicitly with Derrida's general argument about the nature of reason. What it did attempt to do was to destroy Derrida's interpretation of Descartes. In exposing flaws in Derrida's reading, Foucault no doubt intended to insinuate that they stemmed from a false philosophy of knowledge. But this was left all but unstated. For Foucault's response to Derrida's general interrogation, we have to take a rather wider view of Foucault's work, and in order to do this, I will focus on certain key essays. But let us begin with Foucault's defence of his reading of Descartes.

Foucault saw that Descartes no longer saw madness as a permanent threat, and that he dismissed it summarily from thought. Foucault also saw that this dismissal was a precondition for the emergence of a supreme secular reason from which there could be no appeal. Derrida retorted that madness was not dismissed from thought, but rather that it was overcome within thought. He argued that what Foucault thought to be a final dismissal and exclusion was merely a postponement, on methodological grounds, of the real confrontation with madness, this confrontation taking place with the hypothesis of the malign genius. For Derrida, then, reason was already established by the seventeenth century; indeed the attempt to look before or beyond reason is fundamentally impossible, and is based on the acceptance of a myth – the myth of a true origin.[15]

Foucault begins his defence by noting Derrida's view that the dream has a double advantage over madness as an instrument of doubt: first, the extravagance of dreams can exceed the absurdities of madness, and second, the habitual nature of dreams makes the suggestion that one might be dreaming much less fantastic than the idea that one might be mad. It is here that Foucault seeks to establish the first of *two cases of discursive inattentiveness* on Derrida's part. He argues that the two aspects of the dream, their potential extravagance and their habitual nature, must be kept separate. As far as the extravagance of dreams is concerned, he thinks Derrida is wrong to argue that Descartes saw the dream as potentially more extravagant than madness. Descartes never says that madness is either intermittent or limited. Foucault is well aware that Derrida takes the normality of dreams to be paramount. It is the fact that we all dream regularly that produces bewilderment when we take seriously the proposition that we might be dreaming *now*. The crucial thing about this bewilderment is that it does not prevent the process of doubt being continued. Noting Derrida's view that Descartes does not deal with madness at this stage, Foucault asks us to pay attention to the dialogue between madness and the dream which *is* set up in Descartes' text; madness is an external state with which the possibility of comparison is suggested, the dream on the other hand is an internal state of the doubter; the scenes of madness are fantastic with bodies made of glass or shaped like jugs, while those of the dream are ordinary and here and now; the test of dreaming is applied, and that of madness is just about to be when the shout goes out: '*But these are madmen!*' For Foucault, then, Descartes does exclude madness at this point, and this exclusion is a considered one. Foucault's judgement here does not depend only on the logical point that a philosopher cannot reason whilst mad, nor does it depend only on the practical point that imitating mad people will not convince me that I am mad (while thinking that I may be dreaming may convince me that I really am asleep), it rests also on the very words that Descartes uses. He employs three Latin terms to speak of people who are mad: *insanus*, *amens* and *demens*. *Insanus* is a descriptive term; someone who is *insanus* suffers from illusions and delusions. The terms *amens* and *demens* are juridical and disqualifying terms affirming what the insani are unable to do.[16] What they are unable to do is see clearly, and this is precisely what Descartes has set out to do. Thus the *insani* do not have what Descartes must have; that is the ability to search for the truth.

In this deepening of the argument that Descartes excluded madness from thought, Foucault seeks to demonstrate that Derrida has not paid attention to the care with which Descartes considers and then decisively rejects madness. Before commenting on the reason for Derrida's overlooking of these important textual differences, Foucault will show, in a second demonstration of discursive inattentiveness, that this is not an isolated case. He leads us into this by noting that Derrida would appear to have a rather sharp reply to this restatement of the Cartesian exclusion, and this would be to ask how Descartes was able to speak of the 'extravagance' of painters if he had really dismissed madness from thought. Foucault has two comments to make on this hypothetical response. First, just because Descartes excluded the possibility of himself being mad does not mean that madness cannot be an object of reflection (it will be noted that by writing that madness can be an object of reflection, Foucault effectively withdraws from the self-admittedly impossible project of an archaeology of silence). Second, agreeing with Derrida's insistence that careful attention must be paid to Descartes' Latin, Foucault finds it astonishing that Derrida did not notice that the word 'extravagance' was an addition by the translator, and yet Derrida had written of Descartes' 'express' use of the term.

With two compelling demonstrations, then, Foucault establishes Derrida's carelessness. This is a particularly damning indictment of someone who has been nicknamed '*Monsieur Texte*' (Hartman, 1975, 1976).

Foucault now goes on to give Derrida a few tips on how to read the *First Meditation*. It is important to grasp, Foucault advises, that the *Meditation* is a sequence of discursive events, modifying the meditating subject at each turn, and finally producing a subject whose confidence in knowing the truth of things is guaranteed by God. Thus the *Meditation* is both rule-governed as discourse and constitutive in the sense of producing and modifying subjectivity. In Foucault's phrase, the meditation is both 'system and exercise'.

For Foucault, the consequence of Derrida's inattentiveness is that he is forced into two fundamental errors. First, while arguing that Descartes did not exclude madness from thought, Derrida simultaneously duplicates the Cartesian exclusion three times over. First exclusion: for Derrida, madness is raised by *another* subject, not Descartes himself but his interlocutor. Second exclusion: madness is raised from another place, not the place of philosophy, but the place of common naïvety. Third exclusion: this madness, raised by another from another place, is dismissed, to be replaced by the suggestion that one might be dreaming. Having shredded his own argument by triply dismissing madness, Derrida now has to make further mistakes in order to retrieve the situation. Foucault's case here is that Derrida's position is somewhat similar to the situation that liars might find themselves in, needing to lie further in order to protect the first untruth. So, having committed this first error in duplicating the Cartesian exclusion, Derrida must now commit a second error. For his argument is that Descartes did not dismiss madness (the deep reason for holding this argument is that *nothing* can be allowed to escape the philosophical orbit), and he must now bring it back in. For Foucault, Derrida must now find madness where it cannot be found. The only option which Derrida has, and which he takes, is to argue that the confrontation with the malign genius is the true confrontation with madness. Foucault sees this stratagem as complete nonsense. Far from being 'engulfed by his own fiction' (Felman, 1975, p. 221) the meditator remains cunning, resourceful and in control while confronting this deceiving spirit. This is no real confrontation of subjectivity and madness, it remains a question of holding it off.

Foucault's judgement, at the end of this limited reply to Derrida's lecture, is that Derrida reduces discursive practices to mere textual traces, to marks for a reading. He declares that such work is pedagogically dubious, teaching falsely that the text is all and the philosopher is its supreme commentator.

Michael Sprinker (1980, p. 77) glosses Foucault's conclusion as follows:

> Like any orthodoxy, as Foucault has done so much to show, Derridean deconstruction closes off many avenues of thought; it excludes certain kinds of statements and

certain kinds of inquiry (for instance, the archival work that one associates with Foucault), claiming absolute priority for exegesis, for reading and interpretation which are produced by no other forces than the collision of text with reader.[17]

Sprinker goes on to assert (p. 92) that 'Derrida is simply unable to account for the power that the texts acquire and deploy in the political and cultural sphere, where the play of signification becomes a deadly serious game in which human subjects are at stake'.[18] John Frow (1986, p. 216), while agreeing that Derrida is right to ask how Foucault can go beyond reason, agrees with Foucault's verdict, holding that Derrida's position is pedagogically inconsequential:

> The gesture toward the 'historical situation of logos' indicates the most banal, the most *philosophical* equation of the state of the real with the developed state of reason; and it robs Derrida's question of all its potentially *political* force.

For Edward Said (1978), the debate concerns two 'exemplary positions' and contrasts 'a criticism claiming that *il n'y a pas d'hors texte*[19] and one discussing textuality as having to do with a plurality of texts, and with history, power, knowledge and society'. Echoing this view, Peter Flaherty (1986, p. 165) writes:

> In [Foucault's] stinging final attack on Derrida's method, we can see the extreme tension between 'textuality' and 'discursivity' as rival reading strategies. While Derrida feels that the text must be relentlessly 'deconstructed', so that its network of 'traces' can be better exposed as trapped within the 'prison-house' of logocentrism, Foucault takes the position that a text can be best read against its context, that is, as part of a larger set of discursive practices that inform the *episteme* of its specific spatio-temporal configuration.[20]

Most of the commentators, then, agree with Foucault's remark that what is in question is the issue of whether anything can be anterior to the text, whether there can be anything beyond philosophical discourse (Foucault, 1979, p. 10). If philosophy can and does cover everything, as Derrida seems to hold, then the reign of the philosopher is secure. Foucault will not accept such a position as a truth, seeing such an argument as a legitimation of philosophical supremacy. As d'Amico (1984, p. 176) puts it:

> Foucault argues that Derrida has tried to preserve for philosophy and has revived the classical function of criticism, namely, to protect philosophy from its determination by social and historical forces.

The question that must be asked of Foucault's conclusion, and of those secondary commentaries which support it, is how adequate a response to Derrida's critique is this? How much more than mere assertion is it to hold that Derrida is trapped inside a kind of hermetic textuality, from which position he is unable to confront issues of power and history? Is not some kind of suspicion raised by the fact that Foucault's direct response to Derrida, 'My body, this paper, this fire', only addresses the interpretation of Descartes, ignoring the issues of historicity raised in the first half of Derrida's lecture? In order to investigate these matters thoroughly, we must consider Foucault's *other* replies.

To begin with, what is the significance of Foucault's suppression of the original preface to *Histoire de la folie*? It will be recalled that Derrida took exception to Foucault's determination, marked in that preface, to know madness itself, to investigate madness without repeating the original exclusion and betrayal of madness by post-Cartesian reason. Foucault's project was styled an 'archaeology of silence', and Derrida responded that such a project was impossible. Foucault apparently agreed. For he excised his Utopian aspiration to know a higher reason than that which excluded madness, and he did this by replacing the original preface with a critique of the very idea of a preface. In just two pages, Foucault argues against the tyranny of a preface which would instruct the reader how a book is to be received, and against the power of an author to insist that the work is of one kind rather than another. Between these few lines, a further response to Derrida can be read, as Foucault effectively declares the naïvety of a reader who would treat a preface as inextricably connected to the work that it prefaced. Foucault could neither write a new preface, nor authorize the repetition of the old one, for in either case the preface would interfere with his stated aim of allowing a book to consist just of the phrases of which it is made. This is a double indication of a pessimistic turn in Foucault's thought. On the one hand, the original preface looked to find a discursive form that would not exclude, and the suppression of that preface appears to be a kind of resignation to the fact that such a form will not be found. On the other hand, Foucault is clearly now unprepared to point anyone towards one reception of his work rather than another (although it must be admitted that the large number of interviews that Foucault has allowed to be published do rather detract from the claim that he is against the tyranny of the author), and this does seem to amount to a certain reluctance to be political, a reluctance which is somewhat at odds with the majority of views on the Foucault–Derrida debate which see the strength of Foucault's position residing in its preparedness to put questions of extra-textual power on the agenda.

The suppression of the original preface is not the only alteration which marks the second edition of *Histoire de la folie*. In addition to producing a new (counter-) preface, Foucault also added two appendices. The first of these we have already discussed, it is Foucault's reply to Derrida on Descartes: 'My body, this paper, this fire'. We have not yet touched on the second appendix, a paper entitled 'La folie, l'absence d'oeuvre' which Foucault first published in 1964.

The basic theme of 'La folie, l'absence d'oeuvre' pertains to the relation between madness and silence. Foucault repeats that madness and mental illness have become separated. Madness as other than mental illness is not recognized, while mental illness has become the province of the pharmaceutical companies and of hospital disciplines. But just because non-pathological madness has all but disappeared does not mean that its threat has vanished. The threat remains, and at this point in our history it is the threat of absolute emptiness, the fear that there might be a fault in the fabric of being through which one might fall into unutterable strangeness. Foucault points to the universal phenomenon of the taboo. One must not go on to the sacred mountain, or, like Oedipus, marry one's mother. But these things can be spoken of. Madness, however, is the contemporary Western taboo that we do not even know how to disobey. As the possibility of communicating across the divide between reason and madness recedes further and further away from us, we are less likely to find an understanding of the meaning of our culture. To know who and what we are, in this ordered post-Enlightenment epoch, it is even a liability, and an evidence of instability, if we recognize the depths beneath us.

We cling to the mountainside by our fingernails, but we can no longer articulate the sense of danger and otherness that attends our human existence. The danger is not past. Who is to know, asks Foucault, what transformations are being undergone within this other dimension that we deny, and at what point there will be a devastating irruption into our sanitized and scientized world? Freud gives us the ghost of an indication, suggesting that beneath our conscious minds, something has been repressed, emerging only in distorted form. Foucault has no great admiration for the scientific edifice of psychoanalysis, but he recognizes, in some ways, that Freud is a fellow spirit, a thinker who is concerned with what reason has suppressed. For both Freud and Foucault the truth and meaning of Western civilization cannot even be approached without in some way retrieving what we all, with unconscious duplicity, deny. But Foucault's fear is that madness cannot be recovered, that a dialogue such as the Greeks had with hubris cannot now be had with madness. What for Foucault makes the situation so desperate is that reason has all but surrendered interest in otherness, and its arrogance may well be punished at some time in the future. For 'an experience is being born which will put our thought in the balance; its imminence, already visible but absolutely empty cannot yet be named'.[21]

There is a pessimistic atmosphere pervading this appendix. A certain despair and ignorance work together to place the future of Western culture in the balance. As a reply to Derrida, Foucault gives not a detailed argument but a mood of regret and helplessness. The subterranean optimism which marked the first edition of *Histoire de la folie* has disappeared; only the fear remains.

There is really only one point at which there is something which might be construed as a direct response, and this concerns Derrida's notion of the dissension. For Foucault seems to say that it is an internal cleavage which marks Greek thought in respect to otherness; and this dissension is what, since the seventeenth century, we have lost. It is the final dismissal of madness, the destruction of 'homo dialecticus', that marks our tragic condition. This is the subtlest statement that Derrida is wrong to think that there can be no outside of reason-in-general. Would, Foucault seems to say, that such were the case. Then there might be some warning of what is to come. All Foucault can think is that the realm of silence which now enshrouds madness, this emptiness of which we know nothing, is the site of an unnameable threat. And both the silence and the magnitude of the threat are the work of Enlightenment reason, which even now is completing its coverage over the whole of the human race.

In some ways, all of Foucault's writings may be seen as a series of attempts to evade the logic of Derrida's position. The principle of discontinuity which regulated *The Order of Things* affirms the possibility of absolute difference between forms of knowledge and culture, and then goes on to probe the possibility of nevertheless comparing such different worlds. *The Archaeology* presents an uncompromising attack on the ruling ideas of 'rationalist' history (ideas such as teleology, origins, continuity, objectivity and historical truth), as if in search of a form of historical inquiry that would evade the difficulties which Derrida had so unhelpfully pointed out. *Discipline and Punish* looks to the regulation of time and space as a mechanism for the general and specific location of embodied human beings within particular forms of society, and this innovating approach may also be seen as an attempt to break the bounds of previous ways of speaking about modes of social existence, an attempt which also might provide some kind of key which would open the door out of the restrictive enclosure of Enlightenment reason. The first volume of *History of Sexuality* investigates the discursive preconditions of a particular period of historical repression, with a view to exploring the limits of the power of discourse as against the power of reason. Finally, the second and third volumes of *The History of Sexuality* take us back to the Greeks, once again in pursuit of a way of confronting otherness. This is quite a litany, and it is not proposed to present detailed argument in support of the view that all of these texts constitute a trying out and stretching of reason. We will, nevertheless, be looking in some detail over the next chapters at *Discipline and Punish* and the second volume of *The History of Sexuality*.

Apart from *Histoire de la folie*, however, perhaps the most determined of Foucault's attempts to think through some of the problems and issues involved in what Derrida has characterized as the project of exceeding reason have been his efforts to explore the idea of transgression. A consideration of Foucault's key essay, 'A preface to transgression', will demonstrate that there was no reply to Derrida's general criticisms regarding historicity and reason because Foucault had already conceded the force of his opponent's case. The exclusion of madness was to be seen as an operation within reason.

The Question of Transgression

Foucault's essay 'A preface to transgression' was published in 1963, some two years after the publication of the madness book. It cannot be taken as a direct response to Derrida's critique, but there is little doubt that even before the date of Derrida's lecture, he was aware of some of the arguments that were going to be made against his book. As we will see, his tone in the essay is still characterized by that combination of romanticism, nostalgia and pathos which marked *Histoire de la folie*. Furthermore, since what he has to say in the essay is grounded in a certain cultural sensibility rather than in archival research, his writing here may appear almost Delphic.

The opening passages of the text point to a link between madness and sexuality: both in some sense have been exhausted. As Foucault puts it, echoing his understanding of madness as 'l'absence d'oeuvre', 'Sexuality points to nothing beyond itself.'[22] We are, thinks Foucault, living in a world which proclaims the death of God and which evidences a familiar contempt for nature. The evacuation of the religio-sacred sphere, the suppression of the positive aura which once sur-rounded madness, and the explosion of sexuality beyond a natural reproductive function are all connected. The nature of this connection is that without divine, natural, or symbolic limit there would no longer appear to be the possibility of absolute sin. All infraction can henceforth be only secondary, cause for momentary alteration in the order of *this* world, disobedience defined by human laws of infinite plasticity. There would be no outside to such a world. All difference would be brought back in order to be made once more a part of the same. This would be a world marked by an arrogant confidence in its ability to explain and recover everything.

How could profanation in such a world be possible? The philosopher would reply that the very concept of profan-ation would not be valid within such a world. But Foucault, suspending philosophical logic, is determined to think beyond thought. Even though there is no longer any positive meaning behind the idea of the sacred, suppose that the form of the sacred remains, awaiting recomposition? Would not such a recomposition of the sacred only be achieved by some scintillating transgression whose content we could not even guess at? This is the territory which Foucault wishes to mark by the name of transgression: magnetic, wonderful, unnameable, and waiting to reveal the face of the absolutely unacceptable. His thought is that this face could be our face in an *other* mirror, not the face of the other seen through our mirror, the mirror of reason.

Foucault sets out, then, a dialectic of limitation and limit-lessness. 'The death of God leads to an experience in which nothing may again announce the exteriority of being' (PT, p. 32), and yet if we are not freed from the limitlessness that seems to be promised through this destruction of all exteriority, are we not doomed to an existence of pure anomie? With nothing greater than we are, nothing beyond us to provide a source of meaning, where is the value in existence? Nietzsche's answer to this Durkheimian question is that we can, if we have the will, live purely for ourselves, inaugurating our own regime of difference. But, at the same time as our springs of transcendent meaning have dried up, are we not trapped in a social interiority which will endlessly extend to reincorporate us no matter what we do? Perhaps, from out of this strange sorrow at being a prisoner of infinite plasticity, there is only one spark of joy, which is that there might be moments of freedom. During these moments, will it not be as if the fugitive is forming, enlarging, shaping the social interiority from which definitive escape is never possible? As Foucault puts it:

> The death of God does not restore us to a limited and positivistic world, but to a world exposed by the experience of its limits, made and unmade by that excess which transgresses it. (PT, p. 32)

The idea of transgression which Foucault is seeking to develop here is not dependent upon some notion of transcend-ence. In this respect, there is a respecification of the hopeful desire to know what madness knew and to be where madness went. There is a recognition that we can occupy no space other than our own. But there remains here the thought that this interior space, our sociality if you will, is not fixed. It can be exceeded, and even if this excess will always be incorporated, the thought of further excess remains. Foucault writes:

> Perhaps one day [transgression] will seem as decisive for our culture, as much part of its soil, as the experience of contradiction was at an earlier time for dialectical thought. (PT, p. 33)

There are those – Marxists, theorists of post-industrial society – who would argue that this notion of transgression is merely a redescription of the dynamic of social and technological development characteristic of capitalism. But Foucault, at this point, is much more interested in coming to an understanding of the idea of the limit, and in asking what kind of space does transgression actually open up. Foucault is much more concerned with the drawing of an ontological map than with the mapping of the social – at least in this essay.

The notion of an uncrossable limit makes no sense. Foucault knows, however, that to speak of crossing a definitive limit would express an idealist commitment to a transcendent realm. Such a commitment would be incompatible with his belief in the death of God. For, on his ontological map, the place of the transcendent is precisely the place of God. The only conclusion which he can reach is that transgression is precisely the experience of the limit. 'It is likely,' he writes, 'that transgression has its entire space in the line it crosses' (PT, p. 34). But the boundary has moved. Existence is not now to be seen as circumscribed by a closed circle, with an absolute difference between inside and outside (as perhaps was the case in his conception of the pure otherness of madness). It is now to be seen as 'a spiral which no simple infraction can exhaust' (PT, p. 35). Within the terms of such an ontology, Foucault can quite properly say that otherness lies ahead; and, as Donald Bouchard points out (PT, p. 34), this is how we should understand Foucault's statement in *The Order of Things* (p. 328) that 'modern thought is advancing toward that region where man's Other must become the same as himself'.

Having proceeded thus far, Foucault takes pains to emphasize that transgression is not an ethical matter. It is neither negation of present interiority, nor desire for a counter-positivity of the outside. It is what Foucault calls, paradoxically, non-positive affirmation, a notion that would later form the conceptual heart of Deleuze and Guattari's *Anti-Oedipus*. The idea of non-positive affirmation expresses a pure movement across a limit, a movement which neither repudiates the place from whence it came nor welcomes the place to which it is bound. Without meaning to imply any notion of the Return, Foucault writes:

> The discovery of such a category by a philosophy which questions itself upon the existence of the limit is evidently

one of the countless signs that ... we are becoming more Greek. (PT, p. 37)

So we come back to the conundrum of Foucault's statement that the Greek *logos* had no contrary. When Foucault wrote this, he did not fully understand what he himself meant. Now he thinks it is becoming clear: there can be no exclusion. The Greeks somehow knew this to be the case. The exclusion of the mad, which Foucault had taken at face value, was merely the simulacrum of exclusion. If we are no longer to think in terms of closed circles and totalities, but only of limits and the spiral, the exclusion of the mad is merely a displacement, a knee-jerk reaction and refusal of the possibility of thinking of the limit, an attitudinal reflex founded on the new belief that Enlightenment reason meant utter limitlessness. Foucault, however, is not prepared to spell this out. He embarks upon no detailed autocritique of his work on madness.

But he does examine his own metaphysics, albeit in the most abstract and undemonstrative manner. For what he does is to question the time-honoured prestige and adequacy of all dialectical philosophy. He effectively criticizes both himself and Derrida for conducting a dialogue on the basis of the dialectic between the same (reason) and the other (for Foucault, madness; for Derrida, an unremediable absence). The essence of dialectical thought is division. Yet Foucault is now speaking of a world where there are no absolute divisions any longer. The consequences of this state of affairs are intolerable for the subject who is imprisoned by total freedom, a freedom which can only be exercised in that fraction of a second before its exercise is reincorporated into the deadening order of the same. Is the answer, then, to think beyond the dialectical categories of subject and object? If the deployment of such categories issues in such a paradox as the definition of modern existence as imprisonment by a freedom which can never be exercised, had we not better think very seriously about the validity of notions like the subject? Foucault, in fact, tells us that this is already happening:

The breakdown of philosophical subjectivity and its dispersion in a language that dispossesses it while multiplying it within a space created by its absence is probably one of the fundamental structures of contemporary thought. (PT, p. 42)

One might complain at the rather premature nature of Foucault's formulation, suggesting that this is more a promise than a structure of current thought.[23] But the sense of his position is clear enough. And it relates to the so-called death of the subject, to the idea that Enlightenment thought envisaged the exhaustive investigation of all possible objects save one. The sole exception here is, of course, the human subject. A notion so fundamental in its integrity that no analysis of it is really possible: it is the place of the analyser, always apart from the place of the analysed.

What is not at issue is finding something else to take the place of the human subject. As Foucault writes:

> It is at the centre of the subject's disappearance that philosophical language proceeds as if through a labyrinth, not to recapture him but to test the extremity of its loss. (PT, p. 43)

Foucault's far from explicit reply to Derrida's suggestion that there can be no language other than the language of our reason takes the form of a reminder that reason, in so far as we know it, has always been based on the opposition of subject and object, of same and other. This structure may now be breaking down. The consequence of this is a general recommendation not to look for mistakes in the precise formulation of positive, if tenuous, syntheses and explorations (hence Foucault's characterization of Derrida as a 'well-determined little pedagogue'), but to perform a maieutic function and to encourage forth rather than press back. Foucault's search for otherness in madness now appears in a different light. The structure of modern existence is slowly breaking apart; does this mean that madness is returning? Let us face the question and answer it as best we can, without prejudice. Is that how we are finally to see the madness book? Was it the first step in the search for a post-subjective, post-existential self?

From this interpretation of 'A preface to transgression', it seems possible to produce a rather more acute conception of Foucault's project around the time of the work on madness. He was, underneath it all, concerned with finding a conception of the self, and a conception of knowledge which was (to borrow Nietzsche's phrase) 'beyond good and evil'. He was, in other words, looking to understand what knowledge of the self could be like in non-dialectical thought, in the kind of thought that took any opposition between the same and the other to be secondary, to be the result of a contingent exclusion. We can gain support for this analysis from a slightly earlier essay: 'The prose of action'. At the beginning of this essay, Foucault points out that the Christian/Gnostic division between God and Satan, and between the earthly and spiritual realms, has organized our thought for a very long time. In doing so it has established with apparent finality a realm of the Other, the definitive dominion of which belongs to the devil. But, Foucault asks,

> What if the Devil, this Other, were really the Same? What if the Temptation was not one of the episodes of the great antagonism, but the mere insinuation of the Double? What if this duel developed in the space of the mirror? What if eternal History (of which ours is only the visible form soon to be effaced) was not simply always the same, but the very identity of the Same; simultaneously an imperceptible unblocking and embracing of the non–dissociable. (Foucault, 1964, pp. 444–5)

The language may be difficult, but the aspiration is plain to see: what is at issue is the idea that *all* conceptions of otherness (and madness is a prime example), far from being indications of an essential absence at the heart of existence, are signs of a withdrawal, of an exclusion that is to be understood in political terms, *not* in metaphysical terms. Such thoughts on Foucault's part will incline him in the direction of a politics rather than a philosophy; Derrida's commitment to the dialectics of absolute otherness will keep him within the territory of philosophy, or, put another way, within the province of theory rather than that of practice.

The vision of Foucault's work that we now have presents history as a series of political deformations, as, in other words, the variegated story of power. When first articulated, a certain optimism was in evidence, a slim commitment to the possibility of making reason whole again, of curing its deformities. But, taking Derrida's critique as metonymic of a descending cultural gloom, the patina of optimism was scoured from the surface of Foucault's thought. Instead of seeking continually to reincorporate otherness of whatever form into the sameness of – let us admit it – a Utopian reason beyond our own, Foucault turned (after celebrating, in *The Archaeology of Knowledge*, the death of his own barely articulated hopes) to a politics without absolute solutions and to a pragmatic creed of resistance and survival.

Once the figure of the spiral had been drawn, a figure which would allow no exterior realm (for the spiral would snake to engulf any excess), Foucault's capitulation to Derrida's general critique was pretty well predetermined. The spiral dictates that there can be no history against reason and separate from reason. The Cartesian exclusion comes to be seen as a chapter in political history, hardly the founding of reason and history in itself, not an epistemological break but merely 'one of the great events of Occidental thought' (Foucault, 1964, p. 446).

But this is not the end of the debate. We may say that the first round has been won by Derrida, that his insistence of silence in the face of the transcendental has been accepted. But Foucault will now go beyond that to produce an even more radical critique of reason which will become entirely subordinated to history. This too will be a position antithetical to Derrida. For while Derrida's thought will be untiringly critical of presence, of the idea that, for example, the real events of history can be unproblematically *presented* by an historical text; and while this recognition of the essential absence at the heart of the text will force Derrida to be critical of the very notion of history itself, Foucault will write:

> If interpretation were the slow exposure of the meaning hidden in an origin, then only metaphysics could interpret the development of humanity. But if interpretation is the violent or surreptitious appropriation of a system of rules, which in itself has no essential meaning, in order to impose a direction, to bend it to a new will, to force its participation in a different game, and to subject it to secondary rules, then the development of humanity is a series of interpretations. The role of genealogy is to record its history: the history of morals, ideals and metaphysical concepts, the history of the concept of liberty or of the ascetic life; as they stand for the emergence of different interpretations, they must be made to appear as events on the stage of historical process.[24]

As Derrida's critique demanded, Foucault has forsaken the goal of a 'rationality without recourse' and has taken up the standard of a historicity without rationality. This perhaps is Foucault's final specification of the Same, the notion that there is nothing outside of the historical process. With Derrida asserting that there is nothing outside of the text, their opposition – no longer direct – continues, as we shall see in the next chapters.

Notes and References

1 Jacques Derrida (1978), 'Cogito and the history of madness', in his *Writing and Difference*. This paper was originally presented as a lecture in March 1963; hereafter the essay will be abbreviated in the text as CHM.

2 Mark Poster writes:

> Foucault's accomplishments undercut the privileged place of labour as developed by Marx. Foucault's books analyse spaces outside of labour – asylums, clinics, prisons, schoolrooms, and the arenas of sexuality. In these social loci Foucault finds sources of radicality that are not theorised by Marx and Marxists. Implicit in Foucault's work is an attack on the centrality of labour in emancipatory politics. His thought proceeds from the assumption that the working class, through its place in the process of production, is not the vanguard of social change. Foucault may take this as a fact of life in advanced capitalism, or more interestingly, he may be suggesting that the working class is, in its practice and through its organisations (the Party and the union), an accomplice of capitalism and not its contradiction. Radical change may have come instead from those who are and have been excluded from the system – the insane, criminals, perverts, and women. (Poster, 1979, p. 156)

3 Preface to *Histoire de la folie à l'âge classique*, p. xi (abbreviated as HF throughout); see Chapter 1, fn. 1.

4 *Madness and Civilisation* (abbreviated as MC throughout); see Chapter 1, fn. 1.

5 Shoshana Felman takes a much more positive view than Derrida. She argues that the medium for communication with madness is literature:

> In relation to philosophy, literature is, for Foucault, in a position of excess, since it includes that which philosophy excludes by definition: madness. Madness thus becomes an overflow, that which remains of literature after philosophy has been subtracted from it. (Felman, 1975, p. 223)

Although this thesis is attractive, and could be supported by Foucault's use of the works of Diderot, de Sade, Nietzsche and Artaud, it does depend upon accepting the view that classical reason in some sense created madness at the same time as creating itself. The reason that what Felman says is subordinate to an acceptance of Foucault's basic thesis relates to the inextricable connections between literature and philosophy in ancient Greece. The case of Homer's *Odyssey* shows most clearly the interanimation of two forms that had not yet been born as separated from each other. Was there, then, no 'madness' in those times, the clue to that being that there was no 'literature' as such, and is that not what Foucault implies?

6   As Descombes (1980, p. 23) notes, 'The question of the negative is very characteristic of the development of French philosophy.'

7   CHM, p. 43. Bennington's brief analysis of what Foucault means here is most persuasive: 'As soon as the cogito becomes language it becomes the oeuvre which excludes madness in constituting itself.' For an alternative view, see Felman (1975) p. 227.

8   For an interpretation of Derrida's critique of Foucault which emphasizes that Derrida's belief in the inseparability of reason and exclusion is actually a belief in the double inevitability of attempts to exclude and their failure to be perfectly achieved (thus making space for the anti-philosopher), see Frank Lentricchia (1980, pp. 289–91). In fact, Lentricchia's interpretation can be made to harmonize with Foucault, since the latter never claimed that the exclusion of madness was the first exclusion in the history of reason (he wrote, as we have seen, of the exclusions of leprosy, venereal disease and the symbolic role of death). See against this, however, d'Amico's view (1984, p. 169) that Foucault thought exclusion to be constitutive of meaning itself.

Although the acknowledged pathos of *Histoire de la folie* would seem to indicate that Foucault was grappling with the feared possibility that the exclusion of madness might be the first total exclusion, if Lentricchia's view of Derrida is right then Foucault and Derrida could have combined as allies to search out the failures of this exclusion. That they did not is not final evidence that Lentricchia's view is wrong; the sociological phenomenon of academic disputation is more than enough to explain why the opportunity was passed by.

9   CHM, p. 36. While it would be wrong to suggest that Foucault is some kind of modern Hegel, there is clearly an affinity between their respective treatments of reason; Peter Flaherty (1986, p. 158) is quite wrong to suggest that the 'tendency to totalise the social field inherited from Hegel' is foreign to Foucault's approach; the supercession of the totalization by our reason with something *other* is the secret hope that fuels *Histoire de la folie*.

10 D'Amico (1984) is right to point to Derrida's focus on Foucault's historicism, but he defines this historicism in a strange way, as pertaining to Foucault's assertion of a 'reflective' relation between the *First Meditation* and the dynamics of social exclusion. There is clearly some confusion here between historicism and a commitment to structural causality.

11 Michel Foucault (1972), *The Archaeology of Knowledge* p. 16; hereafter this text will be abbreviated as AK.

12 See Foucault's own assertion on this point, and the supporting commentary upon it in Colin Gordon's 'Afterword' to Foucault (1980).

The Cure of Madness by
Hieronymus Bosch
(Prado, Madrid)

The Ship of Fools by
Hieronymus Bosch
(The Louvre, Paris)

The Temptation of St Anthony (detail) by Hieronymus Bosch (Museu Nacional de Arte Antiga, Lisbon)

The Triumph of Death by Peter Brueghel (Prado, Madrid)

Dulle Griet by
Peter Brueghel (Musee
Mayer van den Bergh,
Antwerp)

Horsemen of the Apocalypse
by Albrecht Durer
(British Museum,
London)

Caprichos No. 43 by Goya (British Museum, London)

The Witches' Sabbath by Goya (Prado, Madrid)

13 For such typical characterizations of Foucault's archaeology, see Henning (1982) and Aronowitz (1981).

14 The connection between such a view and the 'post-modernist' distrust of metanarratives (Lyotard, 1984) should be clear.

15 Jean-Marie Beyssade (1973, pp. 292–3) has questioned the whole basis of the debate between Foucault and Derrida. He argues that Descartes does not deal in definitive truths but only apparent truths, and that these apparent truths are used as a means to search out a certain ground for indubitable truth. Beyssade effectively criticizes both Foucault and Derrida for taking the stages of Cartesian doubt as being comprised of definitive judgements, and for failing to integrate the order of Descartes' arguments into the coherence of the *Meditations* as a whole. With some justice, Beyssade seems to say that both are concerned with using Descartes for their own ends rather than in really seeking out what he had to say.

16 Foucault's case here is not quite perfect. His appeal to the realm of the juridical is slightly weakened by the fact that Descartes does not use the general term, *furiosus*, used in Roman law to designate the legally incompetent by virtue of madness. See Neaman, 1975, Chapter 3.

17 David Wood (1985, p. 94) has commented similarly that 'Deconstruction is essentially a kind of formalism because it interprets as symptoms of a metaphysical syndrome ... what are actually the internal reflections of the other historical conditions of a text's production.'

18 Sprinker's language is not hyperbolic here. Feminists understand what is at stake in the realm of signification. The cunning, and sometimes downright brutal, deployment of the signifier 'man' will illustrate the point.

19 'Reading ... cannot legitimately transgress the text toward something other than it ... *There is nothing outside of the text*' (Derrida, 1976, p. 158). Derrida's statement here is not to be taken in an overly simple sense, as we will see.

20 See John Frow's (1986, p. 215) rejection of any methodological procedure that would simply add together an analysis of text and an analysis of context in the hope that such aggregation would produce historical adequacy.

21 HF, 2nd edition, p. 582.

22 Michel Foucault, 'A preface to transgression', in his (1977a) *Language, Counter-Memory, Practice* (edited by Donald F. Bouchard), p. 30; this essay will hereafter be abbreviated in the text as PT.

23 For a very powerful view that the breakdown of subjectivity is indeed well under way, but with the consequence not of a pluralization, but of a further turn of the Enlightenment screw, see the work of Jurgen Habermas on communicative reason, especially (1987) *The Philosophical Discourse of Modernity*, Chapter 11: 'An alternative way out of the philosophy of the subject: communicative versus subject-centred reason.'

24 Michel Foucault, 'Nietzsche, genealogy, history', in his (1977a) *Language, Counter-Memory, Practice*, pp. 151–2.

4 *The Text and the Body*

We have seen that Foucault sought to recall the experience of a mode of being long since excluded from Western society. His best efforts could find only traces of this life of unreason. Suspicions and allusions, in the work of a few artists and writers, were all that seemed to remain of this dimension beyond our form of thought. Foucault's secret Utopianism, his yearning for the Other of reason-in-general, was exposed by Derrida's critique, which completed a process of re-evaluation already begun by Foucault himself. Derrida insisted that there could be no language of the Other which was not at the same time the language of reason, so that any attempt to think beyond the confines of reason-in-general was doomed from the start. Foucault's reaction to this rebuke was to characterize Derrida as merely the last in a long line of philosophers all of whom asserted the unsurpassability of reason. But, in certain respects, Foucault's response was unfair. It neglected to specify the overall nature of Derrida's project. Foucault was not prepared to see that Derrida's critique was more a questioning of strategies than of overall intentions. To examine this further, we need to ask about Derrida's work, and to raise the vexed question, what is deconstruction?

Deconstruction

Derrida invented a philosophical strategy which opposes reason from the inside. He is not explicit about the motivations behind this guerrilla warfare against the Enlightenment heritage. He has not made repeated accusations about, for example, reason and repression, or reason and evil. A sense of outrage does, however, permeate his work, and the object of Derrida's resolutely theoretical attacks is the dishonest certitude that informs the Western tradition of rational thought. Derrida cannot will himself out of this tradition, but he can expose the furtive assumptions which underlie its arrogance. There is one principle in particular that he concentrates on in order to show how thoroughly unjustifiable it is. This is the principle of, what Derrida calls, *presence*.

What is meant by this term? The answer to this question is not so simple. We can begin to answer it by recalling Wittgenstein's desire for a universal language which would be a perfect reflection of the real world.[1] The perfection of such a language would be marked by its utter transparency. It would in no way obscure or distort the world which it represented. The dream, then, is of one language and one world perfectly attuned. The world represented by the language, unobscured by the language, would be perfectly *present* to the observing subject, who could then *speak* of what was seen.

This dream is much older than the *Tractatus*. It is the inspiration of the natural science tradition, and we can go back, well beyond the Enlightenment, to Plato: the writer of all those texts with respect to which the whole of subsequent philosophy has been seen as merely a series of footnotes. In his myth of the cave, Plato (1941, Book 7) speaks of the journey from darkness into the light, and he tells us that to stand in the light of the sun is to be dazzled by the full and immediate *presence* of justice, beauty and goodness.

Derrida has a double strategy for dissolving the philosopher's dream of perfect communion, through a transparent language, with an unproblematically present world. His first strategy is to show how this dream, or some version of it, has animated the main documentary landmarks of our philosophical culture. Thus he will show that the dream of pure presence, in the work of Plato, Aristotle, Rousseau, Hegel and others, is a deeply complex but ultimately unacceptable fantasy. His second strategy will be to celebrate those marginal texts which express some recognition of the falseness of this philosophical desire for the unmediated truth of the world. This will lead him into the disorienting worlds of avant-garde poetry, experimental writing and those philosophers, like Nietzsche, who write beyond good and evil.[2]

Derrida's strategies operate at a regional level. He is not the eagle flying high over the landscape and mapping the terrain. Rather his thought is like some mischievous lubricant which circulates through the texts he examines, and searches through the cracks into places formerly unknown. He will not, cannot, commit himself to saying what reason is, beyond treating it as somehow within the text. But every text that he works upon echoes the dream of presence, and, for Derrida, the task of deconstruction is to show this disingenuous dream at work.

Why should it be just a dream? Why not a realistic aspiration? This question too can be addressed only at a regional level, by showing, in the course of reading key texts in linguistics, anthropology, philosophy, psychoanalysis, politics and literature, that the pretensions to a pure communion with the world, enjoyed by the author and promised to the reader, cannot be sustained. Let us see how Derrida actually does this in the case of the founder of phenomenology, Edmund Husserl – a key example in view of the phenomenological aspiration to know, without mediation, the essential nature of the world.

One of the crucial distinctions in Husserl's major early work, *Logical Investigations*, is between *expression* and *indication*. Derrida takes these concepts to be the intended foundation of a phenomenology of communication. In other words, these ideas of expression and indication are going to form the basis of the definitive theoretical account of what happens when we talk to each other. Or so Husserl hoped.

For Husserl, a phenomenon can be regarded as an indication only if it indicates something to a conscious being. What is being set up here is the conscious recognition of a physical sign. Suppose we take an example: we should go back into the house because the clouds are beginning to gather. Gathering clouds indicate that it is about to rain, and since we do not wish to get wet we will return to the house. But there is space for the play of interpretation here. If we live in the desert, we may decide to stay outside and celebrate; the poet may not think of the rain at all, drawing inspired words from the shape and hue of the clouded sky; and, again, the gardener may interpret the gathering of clouds in yet another way. The gathering of clouds has no essential meaning; it can form part of any number of sign systems. So, it would appear that there is no opportunity here for a triumphant end to the phenomenological search for essential meaning. What is more, the plural significance of indicative signs does more than affirm the polysemanticism of the world, it also places a barrier between consciousness and reality: the sign system itself will mediate between the two. Thus if the task is to pursue the ideal of an unmediated knowledge of the world, we must find some point where signification does not intervene.

Husserl sought to do this by elaborating his concept of expression. Expression is the term Husserl reserves for meaningful communication. It is the presence of intention behind the communication that makes the communication an expression, an expression of a particular, intended meaning. But can there be expression without indication? Can there be communication of meaning without the mediating interference of the sign? It is important for Husserl's phenomenological quest that he find a place where expression exists in a pure state, freed from the noise of indication. Otherwise how will he sustain the dream of non-mediation? He finds his answer in soliloquy, in the silent interior monologue. Husserl argues that there is no indication in silent soliloquy because the meaning of interior expressions is immediately fully present to consciousness.

What Derrida establishes, then, is that Husserlian phenomenology is founded on two fundamental assumptions: the profound identity of consciousness and thought, and the primordial nature of the voice – that silent voice with which we talk to ourselves. It is from this beginning that Husserl will endeavour to realize the philosophical dream of providing a perfectly transparent account of the essential nature of the world. The word *transparent* is important because the aim is to provide an unmediated account: the question of signification must be dealt with in such a way as to show that interpretive play, arising out of an obscuring distance between the interpreter and the object of interpretation, is not essential. How will Derrida undermine this putative foundation?

We should ask, first of all, what happens when we say something silently to ourselves. We use language, or perhaps form a picture.[3] In both cases there is representation. The language or the picture that we form in our heads *does* mediate between ourselves and the object of our thought; and even supposing that we recognize an infelicity in our thought and go on to reformulate it more adequately, still the form of the representation attests to mediation. Husserl gets around this issue of the ineluctably mediating nature of language by arguing that words are not necessary in an interior monologue:

> In a monologue words can perform no function of indicating the existence of mental acts, since indication would be there quite purposeless. For the acts in question are themselves experienced by us at that very moment.[4]

As David Wood (1979, p. 20) has put it, 'Husserl insisted on the need to conduct his enquiry ... at the level of the expressive signs constituted in solitary mental life, prior to their taking on an external linguistic form'.

There is, then, for Husserl, an imagined moment, prior to the arrival of language, when meaning and consciousness are fully present to each other. But, and this is the crucial point, *this is a moment which we can never know*. For in the attempt to go back to this privileged origin, in the attempt to know what it is we are experiencing at the point that we are experiencing it, we cannot avoid representing the experience to ourselves. Nevertheless Husserl wished to found phenomenology on the secure base of a non-mediated experience of some aspect of the world. What Derrida shows is that such a secure foundation is not available. The experience of the moment of presence is *indefinitely postponed, infinitely deferred, perpetually delayed*. In view of this, why should we take the possibility of presence on trust? Why should we believe in something that we can never know to happen?

Derrida thinks that we should attend to the myth of original presence. It will not be a simple question of destroying the myth wherever it is found. Because, quite simply, the myth of presence – the ideal of unmediated knowledge of the world – is an aspect of the general condition of Western reason. It cannot simply be set aside, as something we can *expect* to get beyond. Foucault tried to do that in the madness book, but Derrida thinks that such a strategy cannot succeed. In his view, the only possibility of internally subverting reason resides in demonstrating the cracks in our understanding which derive from the instability of its foundations. The first project of this kind that Derrida embarked upon pertained to the relationship between speech and writing.

Imagine that the privileged moment of presence is like a sheet of white paper. What Derrida sees is that any investigation of this moment of presence will mark the paper. He concludes that it is not the paper in its pristine state that should be the object of attention, because it cannot be. It is only the marks on the paper that can be attended to. In the beginning, then, was the mark. This mark will be present, but not a secondary presence.

What Derrida shows in his examination of Husserl is that the phenomenological desire to speak directly to the world, repudiating all metaphysical presuppositions, is founded on the assertion of an idealized moment of presence which can never be presented. If, however, we suspend the presupposition of original presence, the focus moves from a pure experience to an experience already corrupted, from a pure world to a world which has fallen from grace, from unsullied silence to the dirty marks of language. But before writing can function as the dominant metaphor of philosophy, there are many prejudices that must be confronted. We will encounter some of them in Derrida's critical campaign against those who subordinate writing to the myth of original speech.

Let us be clear what is going on. Husserl thought the sign, the mark, the word, to be a secondary phenomenon. What such phenomena are secondary to is an originating identity between consciousness and meaning, a pure presence of meaning to consciousness prior to the defilements of language. This is a version of the Cartesian desire for certainty, and Derrida attacks it not as Foucault did because of its political affiliation to exclusion, but because of its untenable metaphysical premises. He attacks it not through the construction of a condemnable historical legacy, but through the analysis of canonical texts which share the same commitment to presence evidenced by Descartes in the formulation of the cogito flooded by natural light. We are speaking, then, of a certain similarity of critical focus on the part of Foucault and Derrida; a similarity obscured by a difference of strategy, and overlaid by a rhetoric of interpretive disagreement. The similarity is not complete, however, because the Foucault of the madness book sought, at a stroke, to go beyond the structure of thought exemplified by Descartes, while Derrida sees only the possibility of making mischief within it. In both cases we are concerned with the problem of change. But the difference is perhaps between the instant discontinuity of revolution and the slow grind of regional reform. As we will see, in the latter part of this chapter, Foucault's *Discipline and Punish* attests to the remarkable changes that may come about through the aggregations of regional reform; and this is something which may help us to understand why, in the overall scheme of things, Foucault moved rather more towards Derrida than vice versa. But let us now see how a general prejudice in favour of live speech over writing is actually a result of the dogged attachment to the dream of presence, a dream which for the moment is Derrida's main concern.

In his essay 'Plato's pharmacy' (Derrida, 1981), which is amongst other things an analysis of Plato's *Phaedrus*, Derrida discovers a hidden ambivalence in Socrates' account of writing. Socrates' central point here is that writing is inferior, a substitution for the original speech/thought. A number of examples spring to mind which support Socrates' view: how many of us have often thought that there is something inauthentic involved in a politician delivering a speech written by others? Indeed, how can a mere reader defend that thought which is essentially another's? As Derrida suggests, is there not something dangerous in writing? Does not writing enable us to feign qualities that we do not possess? If we were to see writing as a gift, would it not be a poisoned gift?

Like all poisons, however, writing may be therapeutic if it is used properly. It is an invaluable aid to memory and communication. Thus writing is ambiguous, indeterminate between good and evil, poison and cure. It is hardly coincidental that Socrates refers to writing as *pharmakon*, a Greek word which can mean either poison or remedy. But, even on the remedial side of this opposition, a question must be put. For a drug is an unnatural thing; something which interferes with nature. This at least was Plato's view. And just as the medicinal use of drug therapy may cause more serious problems than the condition treated by the drug, so we can also see that writing may not strengthen memory at all, but that it may cause it to weaken through disuse – to read one's thoughts at a later date is not necessarily to know them as one's own, nor is it necessarily to know their truth.

The Socratic discourse against writing is directed at the art of sophistry. Just as the sophist may pretend to have knowledge, so might writing simulate truth. Thus, for Socrates, writing is inferior to spoken wisdom, to the felt knowledge of the genuine philosopher. For Derrida it is clear: 'What Plato *dreams* of is a memory with no sign' (1981, p. 109), a memory in direct communion with wisdom and truth. Derrida does not make the connection, but it is clear enough: this direct communion was what Foucault sought with respect to madness. It also helps to throw light on the association of madness and silence; contact with higher reason would ideally be unmediated by the corruptions of signification.

It is not contradictory that the sophists too were suspicious of writing. For them it was a question of effectiveness: live speech is more forceful, penetrates more profoundly into the hearts and minds of an audience. In their case, writing was denigrated because '*logos* is a more effective *pharmakon*' (Derrida, 1981, p. 115). Speech too can enter the mind and work on it like a drug, to poison or to cure. Why should Socratic speech be any different in this respect? How can it evade that fundamental indeterminacy between poison and cure that marks the phenomenon of writing?

Derrida shows that the privilege of Socratic discourse is sustained only through an irredeemable claim of access to a wisdom that cannot be presented, since in its presenting it will always be a question of *re-presenting*; and it is precisely in re-presenting that the undecidable alternation between poison and cure arises.

What is truth except a representation of truth; and because representation is, like writing, an inferior substitution which might also be a false substitution, who is to say that *this* is the truth? The answer must surely be that whosoever claims the truth, claims to reveal it in all the glory of its full presence, claims to mime it with utter faithfulness, must be a magician, a *pharmakeus*. For it is only a strictly magical ability, a hypnotic talent, a supreme cleverness that can persuade us that what we have seen is the light rather than its reflection, the presence rather than its representation. It is, for Derrida, this magic, hypnotic power that since Plato and before has concealed the essential incompleteness of the world. Deconstruction will expose this ersatz magic in its necessarily textual operations. It will teach this:

> The absolute invisibility of the origin of the visible, of the good-sun-father-capital, the unattainment of presence or beingness in any form, the whole surplus Plato calls *epekeina tes ousias* (beyond beingness or presence), gives rise to a structure of replacements such that all presences will be supplements substituted for the absent origin. (Derrida, 1981, p. 167)

What for Derrida, then, is common to Plato and Husserl is a derogation of supplementarity. Within the main tradition of Western metaphysics, what is important is the original presence (for the two examples we have so far discussed: Plato's *forms* and Husserl's *transcendental* ego). The original presence is held to determine its empirical manifestations, its signs, marks, language, writing. The philosophical task has always been to restore that origin, and the philosophical prejudice has been continually to disparage the phenomena subsequent or supplemental to that presence.

Now, the notion of the supplement is essentially ambiguous: a supplement may be a mere addition, but it can also refer to the operation of replacement. Derrida continues his drive against the incoherences of Western thought by examining the consequences of this ambiguity, and he does this through a reading of Rousseau.

Derrida examines what Rousseau has to say in regard to education, sexuality, writing and politics. On each of these topics, he finds that Rousseau invokes the opposition between nature and culture. For Rousseau, the fall from nature into culture is the origin of evil. As Derrida (1976, p. 145) puts it, 'According to Rousseau ... Evil is exterior to nature, to what is by nature innocent and good.' But all is not complete in this natural realm of innocence and goodness. There is, first of all, the condition of childhood, a condition which is marked by dependency. Nurture, cultivation, education, these processes while apparently necessary are dangerous and potentially evil. They promise to complete a certain natural deficiency; but at the same time they threaten to pervert natural innocence. Education, then, is a dangerous supplement. It is unnatural, but also necessary. For the child will die unless it is taught how to survive in the world.

What is this concept of nature that has such a deficiency at its core? What kind of *origin* is this that requires something additional and different for the completion of its perfection?[5] Rousseau's answer to this question is not to recognize the incompleteness of the origin, but to see education as a process whose correct form is already given by nature. Education may be dangerous, but the risk of culture can be averted by drawing the educational model from nature. This seems like a wise response. Except that Rousseau's idea of natural education is found to be as elusive and contradictory as his idea of natural innocence. In particular, Rousseau warns against the threat and perversity of teaching children to imitate. An example may make this clear. The parent wishes the child to grow into an honest, faithful and generous human being. Leaving to one side the profound difficulty that such qualities are cultural, how should the educational aim be achieved? Should the child be encouraged to imitate the honesty of the teacher, or should the necessity of honesty be explained? In either case, it is desirable that the child grow into a *naturally* honest and generous person; but will not the child encouraged to imitate become an actor, and will not the child provided with explanations become calculating? Whether the educational methodology is oriented to imitation or to explanation, there seems to be no guarantee that natural propensities will be developed.

In fact, the form taken by Rousseau's suspicion of imitation prefigures the suspicion of signification that we have already seen in the work of Husserl:

To teach the child true generosity is to make sure that [s]he is not content only to imitate it. What does it mean to imitate generosity? It is to give signs in the place of things, words in the place of sentiments, money in the place of real goods. (Derrida, 1976, p. 204)

For Rousseau, as Derrida points out, one aspect of the child's naturalness resides in the desire to hold on to those things that are valued. To repeat Rousseau's example, 'A child would rather give one hundred coins than one cake' (quoted in Derrida, 1976, p. 204). This is neither greed nor perversity. What Rousseau sees is the perversity of valuing the signifier for its own sake, of valuing, for example, money, power, status in themselves. This will be the danger of introducing the child into the world of signification, a world whose power and attraction were fully appreciated by the author of *Emile*, and about which he wrote: 'Never substitute the symbol for the thing signified, unless it is impossible to show the thing itself; for the child's attention is so taken up with the symbol that [s]he will forget what it signifies' (quoted in Derrida, 1976, p. 266). Rousseau believes, then, that the site of evil is to be found in the world of signification, imitation and representation, in other words, in the realm of *non-presence*. As Derrida (1976, p. 205) explains in his description of Rousseau's position: 'already within imitation, the gap between the thing and its double ... assures a lodging for falsehood, falsification and vice.'

Thus it is that Derrida exposes a profound paradox in Rousseau's philosophy of education. The touchstone of Rousseau's thought is a conception of natural perfection. But this natural perfection requires the supplement of education, and this necessary supplement, instead of transforming the child into a mature adult who will live in communion with a fully present natural world, will introduce the child into a duplicitous culture of imitation, rationality, substitution and signification. If such an introduction is necessary because of a deficiency in nature itself, how can we continue to conceive of nature as the perfect origin, as the full presence to which we must return?

It may be thought that Rousseau was somewhat naïve to try and expound a natural system of education. For quite simply isn't education *the* process of acculturation, the introduction of the subject into history, a history which furthermore actually produces (human) nature itself? Perhaps, as Paul de Man has intimated,[6] Rousseau 'knew' of these conceptual difficulties but bracketed off his knowledge so as to think with a certain naïve clarity. If there are these reasons for thinking that education may not be the decisive proving ground of Rousseau's commitment to nature as the recoverable original presence, might we not find this ground elsewhere? Without putting the matter precisely in these terms, Derrida chose to explore Rousseau's writing on the topic of sexuality.

Rousseau considered himself to be perverse because he was in the habit of masturbating. It is tempting to consider that this self-characterization is explained by contrasting the unnatural-ness of masturbation with the naturalness of sexual intercourse. The latter would appear to be a purely natural act, and as such paradigmatic of the return to nature which Rousseau demanded. Derrida shows, however, that things are not so simple. In the first place, Rousseau's view of the sexual act is somewhat guarded: 'Enjoyment! Is such a thing made for man? Ah! If I had ever in my life tasted the delights of love even once in their plenitude, I do not imagine that my frail existence would have been sufficient for them' (quoted in Derrida, 1976, p. 155). Indeed, Rousseau found sexual intercourse injurious to his health, and regarded masturbation as in some respects preferable, not least perhaps because it provided a source of satisfaction for fantasies which otherwise would have remained unfulfilled. Masturbation, then, is a contradictory activity which both refuses denial and produces fulfilment, at the same time as it confirms withdrawal and signifies frustration. And, as we have just noted, the contradiction of masturbation revolves around the extremely problematic (at least for Rousseau) nature of sexual possession itself. Thus masturbation is an essentially *supplementary* activity, and furthermore the act which it replaces is also supplementary – the pure, natural sexual experience which may even be beyond any human to endure. In addition to this, Rousseau saw his long-standing sexual partner, Thérèse Levasseur, as a substitute for his mother, a supplement to his first love. And what of Rousseau's mother? She was the woman about whom he wrote, 'I never concealed my poor mamma's faults' (quoted in Derrida, 1976, p. 155). Was she not, right from the moment of Rousseau's appearance in the world, a presence which could never be grasped entire, never experienced without mediation, a substitute for and supplement to Mother Nature?

Through his examination of Rousseau's writing about his own sexuality, Derrida finds a chain of supplements never grounded in any empirical origin. From Rousseau's mother, the figure which gave him up so that he would become a self apart from her, to the practice of auto-affection, a supplementary perversity redeemed by the fact that it was only his own self that he abused, the original presence of a pure nature is ever deferred, never confronted. As Derrida writes:

> Through this sequence of supplements a necessity is announced: that of an infinite chain, ineluctably multiplying the supplementary mediations that produce the sense of the very thing they defer: the mirage of the thing itself, of immediate presence, or originary perception ... That all begins through the intermediary is what is indeed inconceivable [to reason].[7]

But Derrida's interrogation of Rousseau on sexuality is finally unsatisfactory. If Paul de Man is right in saying that Derrida missed Rousseau's willed blindness to the irreconcilability of education and nature, it also seems to be the case that Derrida underemphasizes the extent to which Rousseau asserts the total otherness of natural sexuality. Thus the issue that appears to arise, given Rousseau's apparent awareness that the return to the presence of the origin is not humanly possible, concerns the validity of Derrida's general thesis about Western reason's reliance on the model of presence. However, Derrida's thesis is not only that Western reason asserts the impossible, but also that the texts that carry the tradition continually give themselves away and reveal the incoherence of their founding assumptions. This incoherence, and the chain of deferred promises to which it gives rise, is not only present in Rousseau's writing on sexuality. It will also be found in his writing on language.

As with Plato, one of the manifestations of Rousseau's imprisonment within the metaphysics of presence is a disapprobation of writing as inauthentic and derivative. Derrida subjects Rousseau's arguments to careful and extensive scrutiny and finds not only that they are flawed, but also that Rousseau is remarkably aware of the difficulties and paradoxes. It is Derrida's aim, over 150 densely packed and sometimes disarticulated pages, to develop that awareness even further.

We should begin with Rousseau's distinction between the languages of the south and those of the north.[8] In the warmer climate of the south, the people are less constrained by the demands of survival. They do not need to huddle together for warmth or work together to provide themselves with shelter.

They will gather at the water-hole and, if their passions sometimes overflow in exasperation at the heat, or for some other
reason, then that is in the nature of things. For Rousseau, this
is where life begins: in warmth and passion, by the side of the
river. We are before language, which will develop out of this idyll
as song, as the extended wavering vowels which can still be heard
in the voice of the muezzin. The song is, from the beginning,
imitation and representation of the passions. The deepest of the
passions is pity; its music an undulating cry.

But fruit cannot be picked from the trees of the north. In
the coldness of the north, language will arise not from passion
but from need. The social focus here is not the water-hole but
the fire. Rousseau privileges the south as the origin of human
society. But in the north, the social bonds will be strong even
though they are not natural. Social survival in the north will be
the work of developing reason. Language here will not remain
long as merely a mirror for the emotions. It will soon tend, under
the pressure of necessity, towards precision, rationality and the
consonantal stop. For Rousseau this tendency is degenerative
because it will produce enslavement to human reason and the
artificiality of the social system. For Derrida, on the other hand,
such degeneration has always already begun, and is constitutive
of what it is to be a language at all.

It is in the north that a system of laws will develop, a social
contract to place the people in chains. This will arise out
of the general economy of northern existence, an economy
which is determined by a nature which is vicious to beings
who are not in their proper place, who have 'left' that southern
Utopia of laziness, poetry and passion. Rousseau will deplore the
development of the iron conventions of northern life. There was
no need for law in the state of nature, where pity and compassion
functioned to keep the natural social order in a harmonious and
gentle condition. But as northern reason develops so does the
faculty of pity diminish. Law will be needed, and its principle
will not be compassion: necessity is parent to the barbarian.

Thus Rousseau's thought is again marked by the opposition
between nature and culture, in the form here of a division
between north and south. The south is the original home of
humankind, its natural place. It is in the south that simple
communities ruled by a natural law rooted in compassion enjoy
a life of warmth, passion and song. In the north, however, there
arises a barbarism of reason. The northern community fights
against nature, needs to develop laws and a language which will

enable one human being to give precise instructions to another. Would one not then expect Rousseau to hold that writing, that degenerative substitute for the natural voice, first developed in the north? He does not. A separate development, running across the dialectic of north and south, is outlined. It concerns the movement from the gesture to the voice to the hieroglyph. Just as the voice was originally a cry of nature, an expression of passion, so is the gesture also a natural sign: who would need an artificial vocabulary to decode the meaning of a raised club, or of hands covering a tear-stained face? What Rousseau sketches is a double development to the very edge of culture: as the cry of nature modulates into the song, so does the natural gesture lead naturally to the hieroglyph. Rousseau will celebrate song or 'savage' writing just as it serves his commitment to natural order; both form part of the natural language of the passions.

Let us move forward to the Athenian forum, to the public square. Language has by now degenerated. Phonetic writing has emerged as a pale, albeit useful, imitation of the spoken word, its diacritical marks a pathetic attempt to convey the thick sonorities of the voice. Even though we are now a long way from the state of nature, there still appears to be the possibility of a proper mode of being:

> When the orator appears in public, it is to speak and not to show himself off; he represents only himself: he fills only his proper role, speaks only in his own name, says, or ought to say only what he thinks; the man and the role being the same, he is in his place. (Derrida, 1976, p. 305)

The game changes somewhat. Just as the proper place for the first society was the south, and just as the proper form of writing is the hieroglyph, so now the proper mode of being for the citizen is to 'fulfil the functions of his estate'. One origin seems to follow another, natural model succeeds natural model.

What does all this demonstrate? It shows Rousseau motivated by an anxiety at representation. In his imagination he journeys back to the origin of the voice, and finds already that the voice is a representation of the passions. Despite this, he will treat the voice as the origin, hardly admitting to himself that it is a flawed and incomplete origin, but supplementing its inadequacies by reference to the gesture, which was always a sign. Writing, then, will be seen as derivative of the voice, it being conveniently forgotten that the voice which originates rational script was already an inauthentic voice deriving from need's opposition to nature; and to add to the confusion, the most ancient writing – hieroglyphics – will be treated as equally originary with the voice derived from the passions. Phonetic writing will even then not be seen as pure degeneration, because there is a further possible descent into the abyss of reason which arises with the advent of algebra, a writing which cannot be spoken and which can represent anything. Nor is the speech of Western reason entirely unacceptable, since there are both proper and improper modes of its deployment, as is illustrated by Rousseau's thought on, for example, education and politics. Overall, what Derrida uncovers is a series of originating moments all of which are flawed, and all of which have their pre-history back to an origin which in turn has its pre-history. Where does the process end? Certainly not in some lost language before reason, which is the message of Derrida's critique of Foucault, but only in the absolute self-adequacy of God. But God is total unknowability, the absolute outside of reason; and it is to this absolute outside that the schema of presence must always lead, even though the promised destination can never be reached.

Derrida's assessment of Lévi-Strauss will add little to his discussions of Plato and Rousseau, at least so far as the question of writing is concerned. In *Tristes Tropiques*, Lévi-Strauss seems to affirm the primordial innocence of the Nambikwara, an innocence which is attested to by the fact that they did not know writing. But as Derrida shows, this society already had signification. They named things and had proper names for each other, the latter practice of naming being invested with considerable symbolic power as evidenced by the fact that individual names were kept secret and discovered only through the anthropologist's cunning with the children of the village. Thus Lévi-Srauss's assertion that the reality of the symbol was foreign to the Nambikwara is palpably false. What is at issue in his work is a certain inverse ethnocentrism, deriving from the desire for a place to stand from which to observe the rather distasteful truth of the West. The privilege of the Nambikwara lies in their innocence. But, as Derrida shows, there is no criterion of innocence which is adequate to underpin Lévi-Strauss's case. For whatever criterion is selected, it can be easily shown that the Nambikwara are already fallen – into violence, hierarchy, exploitation, in short into signification, and the distance between signifier and signified, exploiter and exploited, leader and led, appearance and reality. But, as we now know, for Derrida there was never a time when that distance did not intervene.

It must be admitted that the prejudice against writing found in Plato, Rousseau and Lévi-Strauss does not appear in their works in the simplest possible way. They are concerned with other things besides the form and functioning of language. We may, then, see the prejudice and Derrida's response to it, in the purest possible state, in the work of someone who was concerned centrally with language. Thus it is, finally, to Derrida's critique of Ferdinand de Saussure that we now turn.

Saussure saw that the connection between the word and the idea it represents is arbitrary. This arbitrary relation between signifier and signified implies two things. First, there is a politics of language: in the absence of natural linkage between signifier and signified, a set of words must be established and thereafter maintained (an original political act and a continuing problem of supervision) so as to allow language to function as a device for communication. Saussure did not dwell on the political implications of his linguistics, focusing rather on the second consequence of his formulation of arbitrariness: the impact of words derives as much from their difference from other words as it does from the referential relationship between signifier and signified. Structuralism, as particularly developed in the work of Lacan, Lévi-Strauss and the early Barthes, radicalized this second implication. Demurring from Saussure's view that signifier and signified are as indissociable as the recto and verso of a page of paper, it was thought to be a mistake to involve the notion of the signified in any rigorous investigation of the production of meaning. The logic behind this position was that the signified can never be confronted except in the form of a representation of it, i.e. the signified will always be a signifier. Pursuing this logic, the structuralists argued that meaning was produced only by the system of signifiers, in other words by a system of differences 'without positive terms'. From this point, the way was open for an exploration of the general properties of signifying systems, and work like Barthes' exposition of the fashion system, Lacan's reformulation of Freud and Lévi-Strauss's discussion of kinship systems may be seen as the result. Such work appeared to break with 'natural' understandings of reality, arguing that the 'natural' is a systemic creation – an argument clearly seen in *Mythologies*, where Barthes defines the ideological mechanism as the production of 'naturalseemingness', and in Foucault's adumbration of epistemic determinism in *The Order of Things*.

All of this can plausibly be seen to have derived in large part from Saussure, although once the message was accepted other harbingers, Marx and Hegel, for example, could be recognized. However, what Derrida saw was that the metaphysics of presence still ruled over structuralism. Reason's tyranny, exercised through the power of notions like determinism and absolute truth, had not been eradicated. It had only been displaced, moved from an atomistically configured and causally powerful real world (whether of material substances or ideal essences) to a systemically configured and still causally powerful ideal world of structures, whose nature could be explored mathematically, and whose reality could be demonstrated through their effects. On either side of the displacement, the availability of the fundaments of the world (whether substances, essences, structures or subjects) was taken as unproblematic, with any difficulties being of a technical kind. Structuralism, then, made no difference to the deep but self-deceptive assumption of Western reason that the original source of reality could be recovered in its full integrity, with neither loss because of, nor distortion through the representational medium. In other words, Derrida saw that structuralism had not abandoned the commitment to an unproblematic ontology, even though at first glance it might have seemed as if the Saussurean formulation and its subsequent derivates had moved away from making assumptions about what there really is in the world.

This critique of structuralism is presented best in Derrida's essay, 'The supplement of copula: philosophy *before* linguistics', first published in 1971. In this essay, Derrida uses Benveniste's critique of Saussure to demonstrate the cultural specificity of the ontological certitude, or otherwise put, the metaphysics of presence, which underlies Western thought. Benveniste saw that Saussure had decided to exclude 'the thing itself, the reality' from his linguistics. But he thought Saussure had been naïve:

> When he spoke of the difference between *boeuf* and *ox*, he was referring in spite of himself to the fact that these two things referred to the same reality. Here, then, is the *thing*, expressly excluded at first from the definition of the sign, now creeping into it by a detour. (Benveniste, p. 44)

Benveniste was aware that the signified exists only as formulated in language, and he suspected therefore that our sense of reality had more to do with linguistic connection than with referentiality. In pursuing this line of thought, he sought to show that the ontological loading of the term 'is' in a sentence like 'This is an ox' is (!!!) culturally specific:

> What matters is to see clearly that there is no connection, either by nature or necessity, between the verbal notion of 'to exist, to really be there' and the function of the copula. (Derrida, 1982, p. 201)

One of Benveniste's examples is the Altaic formulation of 'he is rich', which can be roughly rendered by 'him rich him'. This formulation indicates, as do all uses of the various forms of the verb 'to be' if we think about them hard enough, that the copula functions as a conjunction, as a device of supplementation, and that the ontological function of a word like 'is' is contingent and supplementary to that original supplementation. Thus what this whole scheme suggests, or in Derrida's case underlines, is that our very sense of reality is a product of supplementation. The relation between ego and alter, or between ego and world, is one where the two sides are not radically divided, but where their relation is one of supplementarity: at the same time, *both* ego and world *and* ego supplanted by world.

It is with this in mind that we can return to the first of the implications of the Saussurean theory, to the notion that language is ineffably political; although perhaps it would be better to use the term 'economic' since what Derrida describes is the archetypal economic condition of lack and demand. If languages are systems of arbitrary signifiers which are imposed on a 'real world' which is only experienced ideationally, then, first, the general experience which gives rise to language is an experience of lack, of the inadequacy of the origin; and, second, the recognition of this lack, a representation which inspires the imposition of language in a primordial political act, is already a signification, already a symbolization of an 'out there' by an 'in here', already a language (an arche-writing, as Derrida would say). Thus there was politics before politics, language before language, writing before writing: the origin was never complete unless its name were God, who had designed humanity as a collectivity destined to try and recover what its members had never had, to become, in other words, themselves God.

What Derrida's thought shows is that Western thought, as represented by Platonism, romanticism and structuralism, is founded on a metaphysics of presence; and it further suggests that a major response to the scattered recognitions of the fundamental incoherence at the base of this system is found in all the various forms of the acknowledgement of God. But might not things be entirely otherwise? Perhaps, and more than this cannot be said for we are still within it, the schema of presence is not the appropriate framework through which to understand human existence.

How, then, are we to understand Foucault's *Histoire de la folie* in the light of Derrida's ideas? Simply enough: Derrida is saying that it is certainly necessary to question the Western understanding of the world, but that to question its categorial framework, with a view to stepping entirely outside it, is only to duplicate the structure of the understanding which is in question, relying as it does on an origin and a presence which are utterly unavailable to us.

Foucault's direct response to this work was either evasive or dismissive. But his actual work after the debate shows an engagement with the thickness and duplicity of this world, an engagement which is less obviously tainted by the search for an origin. Some methodological preparation for this can be seen in *The Archaeology*,[9] where Foucault not only admits that his book on madness was 'close to admitting an anonymous and general subject of history' (AK, p. 16), but also asserts that 'Discourse must not be referred to the distant presence of the origin' (AK, p. 25). Lest this apparent capitulation be seen as total, however, it is important to see it in the context of Foucault's continuing rejection of the philosophical road. Not content with playing the role of gadfly to the philosophical tradition, a role that Foucault, somewhat contemptuously no doubt, accorded to Derrida, Foucault would still aspire to burst the bounds of classical reason. But now, perhaps somewhat chastened, he would not think to do it himself. Rather he would look to see where those old limits had been exceeded by the movement of history. And, in detailing in *Discipline and Punish* how social power had become dispersed and 'de-presentified',[10] Foucault leapfrogs over Derrida and reasserts the primacy of the social real over its philosophical reflection. For what Foucault will do, without making it explicit, is to describe one part of the social condition in such a way as to show the critique of presence to be but a belated reaction to social change.

Discipline and Punish

By the beginning of the nineteenth century, the link was broken between Western justice and the slaughterhouse. It is Foucault's argument that torture and public execution became anomalous in the context of an emergent capitalist society increasingly centred on property and the development of the productive forces of capital. The anomaly was expressed in a number of ways. The intermittent but spectacular assertion of the power of the sovereign, affirmed in the barbaric rites of the public execution, was denounced by reformers as tyrannical and inhuman. It was seen as a political threat: not only did public executions, dreadful torture and the humiliations of the chain-gang fail to frighten the masses into law-abiding subjection, as extraordinarily visible events they also actively encouraged the participation of the people in festivals of suspended social order. A new practice of punishment was required, a new mode of penality more appropriate to the demands of a rational social and economic order. Public torture would do little to create a well-ordered workforce. Over the course of less than a century, punishment would come to be seen not as revenge (although doubtless that element cannot be extirpated entirely) but as correction. The aim of the punishment process would be seen as the preservation of a general social order, and the reintegration of 'corrected' individuals into that order.[11]

Foucault's account of this transformation definitely does not take the form of an annotated list of percipient decisions made by the major actors on the politico-judicial stage – we are, in this sense, well beyond humanism and the traditional forms of historiography. He describes a process without a subject, an evolution whose logic is one of functionalist adaptation to macro-contingency, rather than that of an executive committee's response to altered circumstances. Typical in this respect is his discussion of that point in the process at which the dysfunctionality of the old punishment regime was effectively accepted, but at which a clear road towards the new penality was not yet seen. This is a point where advocates of the old order based on the power of the sovereign debated with the reformers whose dream was of a punitive Utopia which would be economically and socially invaluable. Whatever functions such debate filled, it did not arrive at *the* solution. For, as Foucault demonstrates, the general adaptations required by the new social order demanded more than a change in the form and content of punishment, more even than a thoroughgoing change in the nature of the law itself. What in retrospect can be seen to have been required was a whole set of mechanisms for the formation of a new breed of social subject, a new process for the making of human beings. This process, which Foucault tells us did emerge, was not decided upon in debate;[12] nor was it some final triumph of revealed human nature. *There was no unveiling of that which was always present*, Foucault had learned that much from Derrida.[13] No, what appears to have settled the matter in favour of a new model of power and subjectification is (although Foucault does not use this language) the functional viability,[14] and hence inevitability, of the new social ensemble. It all fitted together so very well. The centre of this new process is what Foucault calls *discipline*.

Discipline produces individuals as both its objects and agents. It is not spectacular, but measured and continuous. A technology of observation is essential to it, and the model for this may be seen to be the military camp: a geometrically perfectible site of observation and control. The compelling efficiency of this total environment was gradually transferred across to all aspects of society. It gradually permeated and still remains visible in spheres like urban development, education, health care, the treatment of the insane and the control of criminals.

We are dealing here with the architecture of control, a loom of power which generates knowledge and the potential for the formation of particular kinds of subject. Ideally nothing will escape the surveillance which it makes possible.

It will operate in industry where a new echelon of supervisors will emerge. Under the competitive pressures of capitalist economics, regulation is crucial. Neither waste nor dishonesty can be allowed; but the potential for such leaking away becomes vastly increased as firms grow in size and complexity. Efficient supervision becomes necessary. The emergence of this 'new' supervisory level can also be seen in the schools. With the arrival of the monitor, the tutor, the prefect – positions often filled from among the pupils themselves – the controlling practices become a part of education at the deepest level; they are not merely added on, but seem to be a part of a veritable transformation of essence.[15] Thus the power of surveillance is not possessed as a thing, but rather defines the new field of institutional life. It is a general mechanism known through its effects rather than through its *presence* at a given point. Such power is constant, discreet, but nevertheless corporal in the most subtle way. Its effect will be to develop the individual to previously unknown levels of productive potential while at the same time producing a full acceptance of this new order of social control.

In addressing the question of education and the formation through discipline of new attitudes, it is easy to think that the new focus of attention has become the mind. Although there is no doubt that the new disciplinary regime aims to control the mind, Foucault's point is that it does this by operating upon the body. This is perhaps at its clearest within the prison regime where one can list such legitimized practices as sexual deprivation, the rationing of food and restriction of movement. But Foucault wants to say more than this, and assert that the body is inescapably a political matter. Under various forms of compulsion, it will be required to perform in one way rather than another, to have one set of properties rather than another. It is a force of production, but utilizable only if subjected, trained, shaped. However subtle the machinery of compulsion that is at work, it will always be *physical* compulsion that is involved. As Foucault puts it elsewhere, 'Genealogy ... is situated within the articulation of the body and history. Its task is to expose a body totally imprinted by history.'[16] There is, for Foucault, then, what might be called a political technology of the body, a kind of political science aware of the grossly corporeal nature of social relations. And, although he does not say so, it is this emphasis upon the body that is probably his major response to Derrida's textualism: a demonstration in counterpoint of what he thought to be the latter's inconsequential pedagogy.

Although Foucault may have capitulated, at one level, to Derrida's critique of presence, at another level Foucault finds plenty of empirical instantiations of belief in and experience of *presence as total control*. The main example is the Panopticon, Bentham's model for the perfectly efficient mechanism of surveillance, a technical structure which ensures the unrelieved *presence of the watcher for the watched*. What is at issue here is the historical change from a system of justice, powered by the 'real' presence of the monarch, to a world of oppressive systems whose presence is located in its effects for the new type of social subject.

The Panopticon is very different from the dungeon. It neither hides nor deprives of light. As Foucault puts it, 'Full lighting and the eye of a supervisor capture better than darkness' (DP, p. 200). The convict in the Benthamite prison 'is seen, but he does not see; he is the object of information, never a subject in communication'.[17] The Panopticon, this ever-bright circle of cells facing inward to the surveillance tower at the hub, is a crucial model. It dissociates power from particular people, investing it in a topological configuration of light, bodies, gaze and architecture; as this power becomes topological, it also becomes automatic – residing in the arrangement itself rather than being a contingent addition. The arrangement means that observation can only be perceived as continuous by the object of this permanent examination. This in itself controls the behaviour of subjects who are now 'made' so as to react to such stimuli.

Foucault speaks of the administration of the plague-stricken village as being the beginning of discipline, describing the hierarchization of the plague administration, the systematic sectioning of the stricken community, the regular roll-calls, and the exquisitely detailed recording of every death and every irregularity observed by the patrols. From the plague to the Panopticon, a movement from the extraordinary to the everyday, the panoptic model can be applied whenever the control of people is necessary.[18]

This extension of power is not despotic. Such power is not invested in any single individual. It is a form of power appropriate to democratic ideologies, for a deindividualized power, especially one devoted to the general strengthening of the social body, can be democratically administered by committees elected from the mass of the people. The disciplinary society aims to make useful individuals, and the spread of the disciplinary mechanism from the margins of exceptionality, a village stricken by plague, for example, to the centre of things, to the factory, the school, the hospital, the armed services, derives from the effectiveness of discipline in producing utility.

A fundamental feature of the development of discipline is the deconstruction of the masses; discipline converts the mass into a collection of specified individuals. In the name of increased social productivity and enhanced political stability, the masses are recomposed into an efficient machine, and this applies whether one is speaking of the democratic electoral process, or the prosecution of national defence, or the running of mass manufacturing industry.[19]

This control over bodily powers, this preparation for a great social harvesting, was not achieved by means of a conventional brutality. Through a relentless process of correction, however, new behavioural standards were imposed relating to punctuality and the precise self-regulation of time, to new levels of concentration and norms of earnestness, to forms of dress and personal hygiene, and to interpersonal conduct of all kinds. This process of reformation was assisted by corrective mechanisms which exposed nonconformists to a panoply of effects, from slight humiliations to physical punishment. Even the smallest departure was noticed and acted upon. As the process gathered momentum, each individual found that the social cosmos had become saturated by assessments, punishments and normatively deepening requirements of all kinds. The correction of defects was a means of procuring the development of the subject towards the required state. Such discipline was like a series of exercises repeated over and over until the accomplished playing of this new social music became second nature.

But punishment was only one side of this system of social engineering. Foucault describes a Manichaean universe where one's stage of development could be precisely located on the continuum between good and evil. The dream was that the process of character formation could be precisely charted, specific natures and potentialities assessed, true judgements rendered with respect to all in the system. The place on the continuum, or, otherwise put, the precise judgement (even if temporary, as might have been the case when dealing with those still in the formative stage), functions as a reward or punishment in itself; just as promotion to a higher rank is seen as a reward in itself in the military institution.

The general ideology underlying this total process was one of improvement and progress; the need for regimes of punishment would even gradually disappear as individuals became perfected. The result of the process was the cloning of the subject population, the normalization of the individual. The old opposition of right and wrong would, as the mechanisms of normalization approached total efficiency, disappear. We have entered the age of the norm, and left behind the presence and arbitrary power of the king. The overpowering visibility of the monarch is now replaced by the permanent visibility of the subject, of all subjects, and just as the presence of the sovereign had perforce to be established in the brutal rituals of a central power, now new rituals, product of a power diffused throughout the social body, came forward to secure the *new and mythical presence of the norm*. One such ritual form is the examination which assumes a central place in this new technology of subjectification.

The school is a place of constant examination, in the double sense of observation and testing. If observation was general, the precise calibration of the achievement level of those observed is an even more significant clue to the ways of power in this new order. The examination objectifies even more than the regime of observation. It allows true statements, corroborated by 'evidence', to be made. As if in heed of Plato's theory of metals, or in prefiguration of the functionalist theory of stratification, individuals would thence be justly assigned to their natural places in the order of things. It is also notable that the examination situates the subject within the world of the written and the recorded. The techniques of filing, tabulation and notation were basic to discipline, and to the emergence of the human sciences (by which is meant here the legitimization of the individual as rightfully placed within an epistemological field). The examination begets records; each individual becomes a case; the limit of describable individuality is lowered. The written record is no longer a privilege of those people of note whose biographical details were preserved for posterity; it has become part and parcel of the operation of power. Individuals are documented, and these writings and files are *for use*. Individualization, formerly ascending, is now descending; and as a necessary logical concomitant of the sovereign's disappearance, power becomes anonymous. No longer invested in the king, it can only now be everywhere. Ever present, but never locatable: Foucault's new formulation of power is precisely Derridean, an application of the critique of presence, but done from within an historical sociology rather than from within philosophy.

What is the significance of the police in all of this? It may sanction, in a certain way, the spread of discipline; but it does not arrogate the powers of discipline to the state, even though it extends to every corner of the social body, a potential assessor of every action in every moment of time. Why is this? It is because discipline is a set of techniques that does not *belong* to any particular apparatus.

Discipline is the precise reverse of the spectacle. It exercises power at lowest cost but maximum intensity, producing docility and utility. And is there not a political development also, in terms of governability (see Foucault, 1979a) and the move from administration by force to administration by consent? As Foucault writes, 'Let us say that discipline is the unitary technique by which the body is reduced as a "political" force at the least cost and maximized as a useful force' (DP, p. 221).

Discipline is, in a certain sense, something outside of the law. It cannot be voted upon or contracted into.[20] Its subordinations are beyond fairness or exploitation. As Foucault explains, 'The minute disciplines, the panopticisms of every day may well be below the level of emergence of the great apparatuses and the great political struggles. But, in the genealogy of modern society, they have been, with the class domination that traverses it, the political counterpart of the juridical norms according to which power was redistributed' (DP, p. 223).

The birth of the prison was not coeval with the emergence of disciplinary society. But in defining the power to punish as something exercised by society over all its members, imprisonment came to be seen as a natural penalty, a form of punishment which fitted perfectly into the disciplinary grid. Since freedom was a right for all members of society, it is hardly surprising that deprivation of freedom came to be accepted as the universal standard. It also has the advantage of allowing the operation of a precise penal arithmetic. Furthermore it reproduces the form of disciplinary society itself; prisons are societies in microcosm. It restrains and retrains. Just as the wider society works changes upon its members, so does the prison. The discipline of the prison must be total; it will monitor and regulate all aspects of the inmate's life: aptitudes to work, moral inclination, the state of body and of mind. It will do this continuously, expressing a function of total power. It will do this not least because the prison is a reformatory, not a mere place of exclusion. The method of exclusion, described by Foucault in his book on madness, has been replaced by a technology of reincorporation. Its methods of isolation, enforced work and continual assessment are therapeutic. We might label the process *carceral transformation*.[21]

Seeing the prison in this way enables us to understand how the prison system came to participate in the judicial process. The judge's sentence was only part of the story; if carceral transformation were achieved in less time (there is no discussion of the reverse case where reform is incomplete at the end of the allotted sentence) then shouldn't the inmate be allowed to leave? What this amounts to is that the nature of the offence comes to be only one of the factors which determine length and quality of sentence. The avenue to some autonomy within the penal system for the prison was clearly lying wide open; but the judiciary were hardly happy about this at first. One can see why. Here is a possible new source of arbitrariness, no longer residing in the power of the king who was above the law, but now resting with the prison. In Foucault's terms, we have an 'excess ... of the "carceral" in relation to the "judicial" ' (DP, p. 247). This 'excess' stems from the requirement that the prison have social utility. Foucault refers to this 'disciplinary addition' to the juridical as the 'penitentiary'. This concept is effectively a practical application of Derrida's theorization of the supplement; from the standpoint of the judiciary, doubtless carceral autonomy was a 'dangerous supplement'.

As a therapeutic process, the prison is clinical: a place of both surveillance and recording of knowledge. Panoptical in nature, the prison has to 'transform the penal measure into a penitentiary operation ... from the hands of justice, it certainly receives a convicted person; but what it must apply itself to is not, of course, the offence, nor even exactly the offender, but rather a different object ... the *delinquent*' (DP, p. 251).

The delinquent is not the author of a criminal act pure and simple, rather the delinquent is a life, a collection of biographical details and psychological characteristics. The delinquent is also 'an object' in a field of knowledge, a field patrolled by experts – jurists, but also psychologists, social workers, in short a whole series of professional biographers, whose task has been to change the reference point of criminality from the act to the life.

The generalization of imprisonment was not universally welcomed. From the very beginning there were criticisms (see fn. 21). What is interesting is the way that the standard criticisms were responded to by affirming, *as if for the first time*, determination to put into operation one or more of the features that had defined prison discipline from the beginning.[22] There is an important point to be made here which concerns the politics of reformism, and which begins to provide an explanation of the politics of deconstruction, of the reservations which Foucault and Derrida share regarding 'the political'. The point is that the repetition of the basic components of the prison system, in the form of a programme for reform, instantiates the basic paradox that reform movements tend to reaffirm the basic characteristics of the institutions to be reformed, while revolutionary programmes of change rest on delusionary identifications of ideal models whose presence is located behind the manifest world.[23] For Foucault, this paradox has led to a rejection of 'general politics' in favour of a politics of local intervention. For, as Maurice Blanchot (1986, p. 44) has noted, a concern for the grand design functions marvellously as an 'alibi for everyday servitude'. These issues will be examined in more detail in the next chapter; but in the mean time, what are we to make of the paradoxical situation where the principles of the prison attest to a desire to control delinquency, but where the constant reaffirmation of these principles in response to continual streams of the same thoroughly justified criticisms seems to indicate a wilful blindness, almost a desire for the continuance of delinquency?

Foucault asks how the juxtaposition of desire for delinquency and for its eradication can be explained? He suggests that we should ask what the reproduction of delinquency does. Perhaps prisons are not meant to eliminate delinquency but to distinguish it, distribute it, use it. Is prison a way of controlling illegality, of allowing some forms free rein while branding other forms unacceptable? Wouldn't this reproduction of the form of the unacceptable function so as to prevent deeper unacceptabilities arising? In other words, is it a question of seeing the failures of imprisonment as rather a successful tactic in the ordering of society (and other forms of oppressive stigmatization of difference can, of course, also be seen in this functionalist perspective)? Such a hypothesis is given weight by processes that were emerging at the end of the eighteenth century, and in particular by the association of crime and deep political opposition. The emerging capitalist order was giving rise to harsh regimes. Crime was a way of protesting. It had to be depoliticized. One way of doing this was to find in the lower classes a tendency to criminality and delinquency. It was clear enough that the process of law was most often a process in which representatives of one social class passed judgement on representatives of another. Bourgeois crime was tolerated because it did not threaten social order. The specification of delinquency succeeds in making lower-class illegality 'harmless' to the political order. And there are further reasons for reproducing this harmless delinquency, and these have to do with the way a localized and recorded criminal population may be useful to the bourgeoisie in the facilitation of profit-making from marginal activities such as prostitution, arms dealing, the subversion of prohibition, and drug-trafficking. Furthermore, the criminal population under surveillance constitutes a source of informers, an unofficial army of spies who can be forced, because of their subordination to policing agencies, into the role of social supervision. As Foucault puts it, 'delinquency, an object among others of police surveillance, is also one of its privileged instruments ... The everyday melodrama of police power and of the complicities of crime that formed with power was soon to begin' (DP, pp. 281–3).

Overall, the prison-police-delinquency system deepens the disciplined control of the whole society; it forces everyone into an authorized place within a functioning hierarchy; that place is prison in the event of any serious expression of a desire for freedom from the world of discipline. It is an alliance of Durkheim and Weber: society has in truth become the Protestant God that keeps all under constant observation, and the individual members of the God-Society take this task unto themselves for their own and others' sakes.

It even seems to be the case that the functional necessity of delinquency is effectively accepted, since the notion of a 'disciplinary career', a kind of counter-curriculum which parallels the continuum from minor infraction to major crime with a series of institutions from orphanages to high security prisons, is very much a part of our society. This twin series of graduated actions and institutions works on the basis of a general normativity, no longer on the warrant of a sovereign. No longer will there be horror of essential otherness, everything will be judged in terms of its relation to the norm. As Foucault puts it (effectively acknowledging the correctness of Derrida's formulation):

> The carceral network does not cast the unassimilable into a confused hell; there is no outside. (DP, p. 301)

The delinquent is precisely within the law, produced and maintained there. We live in the universal reign of the normative, a reign inaugurated not by some fictitious contract, but rather unconsciously by the spread of the carceral continuum. This carceral network both objectifies and subjectifies human individuals. It made the human sciences possible, for its outcome is 'knowable man'. It is the disciplinary network that is at the heart of this.

It may be that the prison is not indispensable. At least two contra-indications to the prison arise: first that the 'rustic and conspicuous workforce of delinquency' may be ineffective in the context of national and international crime. Foucault mentions narcotics and financial crimes, but the Mafia and espionage may be even more telling in this regard. Second, 'medicine, psychology, education, public assistance, "social work" assume an ever greater share of the powers of supervision and assessment' (DP, p. 306). Both points indicate that the prison may be losing something of its point and effectiveness. On Foucault's model, however, whatever general changes may take place in the future will not assume their final place within a new functionality as a result of rational decision-making.

Foucault's elaboration of discipline as the new social principle of capitalist society constitutes a description of a social world beyond presence. While society may now have no power-centre, but rather 'a multiple network of diverse elements – walls, space, institution, rules, discourse ... a strategic distribution' (DP, p. 307), and while it may follow that notions of repression and exclusion are thus no longer adequate to understand the workings of this new order, it is obviously not enough to recognize that this was the deep message underlying Derrida's critique. The question must now be posed as to the significance of this 'de-presentified' world; what possibilities for thought and action may now form within it? What are the possibilities for conceiving of difference and otherness within such a world? If supplementarity is the essential social condition, does this mean that alternations between identification and repudiation will inescapably define all relations between social groups? These questions, and others like them, lie behind the anxious search for the political implications of the thought of both Foucault and Derrida. It is to these implications and this search that we now turn.

Notes and References

1 Wittgenstein (1961) wrote:

4.001 The totality of propositions is language.
4.01 A proposition is a picture of reality.
4.05 Reality is compared with propositions.
4.06 A proposition can be true or false only in virtue of being a picture of reality.

For a discussion of Wittgenstein and Derrida which focuses rather more on the former's *Philosophical Investigations* (the mature expression of Wittgenstein's repudiation of the *Tractatus*), see Staten (1984).
2 This division between Derrida's two strategies is not a little crude. But as an introductory heuristic, such crudity is probably necessary. It is worth pointing out that Derrida's writing on such figures as Genet, Mallarmé and Ponge can be more easily appreciated once one has seen the critique of presence at work on the texts of Plato, Rousseau, Husserl and other more conventional writers. Since this book does not aspire to be a total treatment of Derrida's work, the first strategy will occupy the centre of the proceedings in the present volume.
3 It is possible to argue that experiencing an emotion is a form of soliloquy, and this does complicate matters to an extent that neither Husserl nor Derrida is prepared fully to explore. A full exploration of the resulting issues would move us in the direction

of Merleau-Ponty whose concern was, in Paul Ricoeur's words, 'to bring language down to its perceptual and bodily foundation rather than guide it towards its proper field of actualization' (Paul Ricoeur, 'Foreword' to Madison, 1981, p. xvii).

4   Husserl (1970, p. 280). It is fairly clear that Husserl *is* using a model of bodily/emotional states to found his analysis of thought. But, as suggested in the previous note, it fell to Merleau-Ponty to develop the implications of this unacknowledged side of Husserl's thought.

5   It may be thought that Derrida's view of the origin as incarnate completeness is a little awry. The reason for questioning his usage here pertains to the clear difference between the origin and the end state; for that there is, by definition, a difference between the origin and the end would, it might be thought, mean that the origin is *ipso facto* incomplete. Such a view overlooks the point that the concept of the origin implicit in Western thought is such as to require the total inclusion of all developmental potential within the origin. Otherwise the process of development will not be fully accessible to rational understanding.

6   De Man writes: 'Derrida's considerable contribution to Rousseau studies consists in showing that Rousseau's own texts provide the strongest evidence against his alleged doctrine ... Rousseau's work would then reveal a pattern of duplicity ... he "knew," in a sense, that his doctrine disguised his insight into something closely resembling its opposite' (1983, p. 116). De Man's view is that Derrida duplicates this blindness by reading Rousseau as if he were naïve. On de Man's part, this is not meant to be a damning criticism; for 'blindness [is] the necessary correlative of the rhetorical nature of literary language' (p. 141).

7   Derrida (1976, p. 155). It need hardly be pointed out that here is another formulation of Derrida's critique of Foucault's work on madness. Put succinctly, Derrida's point is that Foucault was acute in thinking madness to be 'inconceivable to reason' but was wrong in thinking that madness finds the secret origin upon which reason has always relied.

8   Derrida is well aware of the Eurocentrism involved in using the terms *north* and *south* in the way that Rousseau does.

9   *The Archaeology of Knowledge* (abbreviated as AK throughtout); see Chapter 3, fn. 11.

10 A word first used in AK, p. 47.

11 It has been suggested that Foucault regarded this change as in some way regressive (O'Brien, 1977, p. 510). But by the time he came to write *Discipline and Punish* (abbreviated as DP throughout; see Chapter 1, fn. 3), he knew as well as anyone that there is nowhere to stand from which to make such a judgement.

12 Taking up Jacques Léonard's critique (discussed briefly in Merquior, 1985, pp. 102–3) that Foucault totally ignores some very real and basic mechanisms of historical agency, Heinz Steinart has argued that Foucault undervalues the role of the state in the dissemination of discipline, and also that he does not carry through anything like an adequate sociological analysis of the different interest groups

in French society at the time of the transformation about which he writes. Such criticism should certainly be noted. But it is Foucault's contention that even the most exhaustive inquiries of this kind will still leave such total phenomena of transition underdetermined. Furthermore, the critical allegations of factual omission and strategic neglect made by such writers as Léonard and Merquior are founded upon an unexamined set of assumptions concerning social causation. Unlike such critics, Foucault has sought to examine such assumptions; he has found them both incoherent and politically duplicitous.

13 Both would reject the let's-get-back-in-touch-with-our-bodies kind of thinking, exemplified in the following passage from David Michael Levin (1985, p. 255): 'Thinkers like Foucault concentrate on the ways in which a political regime externally appropriates the human body, imposing its demands on an essentially passive material; and they will explore strategies of resistance suggested by the bodies' experience of political institutionalization. But they neglect to acknowledge the body's own intrinsic political wisdom.'

14 Deleuze (1986, p. 33) has spoken of 'This new functionalism' in his discussion of *Discipline and Punish*; while Fred Dallmayr (1984, p. 86) has written: 'Foucault's disciplinary power is readily compatible (I believe) with the functionalist theory of power, and especially with Parsons' view of systemic integration and cohesiveness.'

15 Merquior (p. 103) suggests that Foucault's picture of educational discipline contradicts the post-Enlightenment 'pedagogical effervescence' inspired by such luminaries as Rousseau and Pestalozzi. But notwithstanding Derrida's demonstration that *Emile* testifies to the essential incoherence of 'natural' models of teaching, one of Foucault's main points is that the ideology of the Enlightenment and the disciplinary society are well suited to each other: *everything seen to be in its place* could work as the maxim for either.

16 Michel Foucault, 'Nietzsche, genealogy, history', in his (1977a) *Language, Counter-Memory, Practice*, p. 148.

17 DP, p. 200. Although this is not the place to go into it, it is notable that Foucault's formulation here specifies the precise difference between Habermas and himself. For an introduction to the debate, see Richard Rorty, 'Habermas and Lyotard on postmodernity' in Richard J. Bernstein (1985).

18 O'Brien (p. 516) has noted perceptively that Foucault pays little attention to changes in the family during the period which he examines. A history of such changes, under the sign of the panopticon, has yet to be written.

19 There is a basic disagreement between Foucault and Baudrillard (1983) on the very existence of the masses. Foucault's social constructionist ontology does not lead to theses about the non-reality or simulation of the masses, as it does in Baudrillard's case.

One should also note Foucault's implicit tactical disagreement with the Marxists: the proletariat are wrapped in the disciplinary society, and conceivably must be extricated from it before they could become the agency of revolution.

While on the topic of revolution, Foucault's work raises intriguing questions regarding the state of societies where major revolutions have taken place – could the 'level of disciplinarity' in Russia or Iran, for example, be measured?

20   As Pasquale Pasquino (1986) has explained, while the juridico-political discourse of the seventeenth century was constructed around the idea of 'contract', which presupposes rational individuals as constitutive elements within the contract, Foucault's problem is that of interrogating modernity by considering the way in which these supposedly rational individuals are constructed.

21   It should be understood that this was not something unambiguously appreciated throughout society, nor when it was appreciated was it necessarily approved of. The consternation Foucault discusses concerning the apparently unfair and paradoxical competition provided by prison workshops against 'free' enterprise is just one example of a certain inefficacy in the symbolization of imprisonment. No doubt further research would reveal many other cases where the nature of the prison according to Foucault would not coincide with its nature according to many members of the society that imprisonment is supposed to serve. This is borne out by Foucault's discussion of the standard criticisms made of imprisonment right from its inception as the typical punishment. These basic criticisms were that prisons do not reduce the crime rate, they cause recidivism, they produce delinquents because they are unnatural places in which feelings of injustice make individual reform impossible, and in which the encouragement of informers creates an atmosphere of unavoidable corruption, they also provide a criminal milieu, a sub-cultural location, a counter-education, and they leave the residue of the police record (or the then equivalent) which of itself, in its social effects, makes recidivism almost automatic; finally they force families into vagabondage because the head of the family is withdrawn. (See DP, pp. 265–8.)

22   The seven basic features which would re-emerge, in a 'utopian duplication' (DP, p. 276) were the principles of correction (reforming people), classification (separating different kinds of offenders), modulation of penalties (rewarding the achievement of reformed behaviour), work as obligation and right, education, technically well-qualified staffing, and the provision of auxiliary support institutions to help the ex-convict.

23   See the discussion of this point in Carroll (1982, p. 193).

5 Post-Hierarchical Politics

Derrida's critique of concepts has supportive implications for the rethinking of possible forms of social organization which is only now just barely taking shape in, what we might refer to as, radical discourse. In feminist thought, in critical Marxism, in anti-racialism campaigns, in workers' co-operatives, in the more innovative sectors of commerce and industry, even in some parts of national and local government, many of the questions which arise stem from the same basic issue: how can difference be managed? The sense of the question is only just beginning to emerge, and it will not do so fully without a struggle. The reason for this is that all the arenas in which we exist are structured in accordance with, or in counterpoint to, one dominant social model. That model is the hierarchically ordered bureaucracy. Because of the grip that principles such as order, efficiency, predictability, goal achievement, role definition, planning, differential status, differential responsibility and differential reward have on our daily lives, in both personal and institutional contexts, and in ordinary or extraordinary situations, we find it almost impossible to think about difference without reducing it to variations upon that one original theme of which we ourselves are but a variation.

But are hierarchies really necessary, and if they are, do they need to take the kind of form handed down to us from the Roman army? It cannot be pretended that there can be a definitive answer to that question. From a theoretical standpoint, an answer could only be provided from outside of our form of reason, and we now think that there is for us no such place. From a practical standpoint, while it may be the case that hierarchically principled society must either exclude or nullify pure difference, it is nevertheless the case that the principle of hierarchy, and all that goes with it, does not equate to totalitarian terror: bureaucracies and hierarchies offer security, predictability, a home for ambition, and a superlative if tightly constrained mechanism for goal achievement, at the same time as they may reproduce a culture of stultification, oppression and inequality.

What this chapter seeks to do is both to document the final stage of the Foucault–Derrida story, and to ask about the politics of their work by focusing on the relation between reason and hierarchy.

Difference, in the West, has come to mean the absence of value. This is one major significance of Foucault's history of madness, that it explains the mechanism which underlies this loss of status for whomever seems radically different. This absence of value means that a threat exists, a threat from a place which is not locked within the societal hierarchies. Difference is a threat because it is beyond comprehension and, if allowed to be what it is in its own alien otherness, it is outside of the control mechanisms which are well established for those subjects who are firmly part of the societal hierarchies. There are two logical strategies for dealing with such a threat: exclusion, on the one hand, and neutralization and incorporation, on the other. Foucault's work suggests that the latter is by far the most common. As a general rule, difference will be neutralized and incorporated. In truth, does not such an objective destiny lie in front of most social movements which pursue equality for this group or that? Resistance, from the upper echelons of the societal hierarchies, to such movements will probably come to be seen, within the future history of our culture, as ignorant and short-sighted. After all, neutralization and incorporation are key strategies of contemporary sociopolitical control. But there are still those who wish for a form of thought that promises affirmation and invitation, instead of neutralization and incorporation, as a framework for accommodating difference.

Derrida's thought is relevant to this complex set of issues because he exposes the insubstantiality of the ground upon which people think themselves to stand when they say that there are no alternatives to the hierarchies which structure our lives, in sometimes harsh and wounding ways. One of the most important implications of Derrida's critique of presence is that it leads to an appreciation of hierarchy as illusion sustained by power. It may be a necessary illusion, at our stage in history. We do not know. But there is no rational warrant for assuming that other imaginary structures would not be possible.

Foucault's thought is relevant since it confronts the inescapability of power at all levels of social life as we know it; and even if Foucault's shift from the hidden optimism of the madness book to the more open scepticism of *Discipline and Punish* may be seen as ideologically inadvisable by those who seek a better world, there is no doubt that his later thought is tinged with a more biting political and psychological realism. Such hardheadedness will undoubtedly be necessary for anyone who accepts the challenge of thinking within our system of thought (which is inevitable) but against the deepest social conventions.

Derrida's argument against the false privilege of presence, against the delusive certainty that representation is secondary and somehow inessential, against the unfounded belief that the domain assumptions of our culture are as natural as cold in winter and warmth in summer, can be restated as a critique of all the categorical oppositions of Western thought. Binary pairs such as intelligible and sensible, inside and outside, good and evil,[1] truth and falsehood, heaven and earth, nature and culture, speech and writing, capital and labour, man and woman, white and black, are, if seen through the lens of Derrida's critique of presence, not simple alternatives. It is rather the case that one side of each opposition has a presumed privilege over the other. One side is original, the other side secondary, derivative, worth less. As Derrida (1981a, p. 41) has put it, somewhat formulaically (Spivak, 1976, p. lxxvii): 'One of the two terms governs the other ... To deconstruct the opposition ... is to overturn the hierarchy at a given moment.' Deconstruction, then, in this somewhat mechanical formulation, means reversing polarities, and according privilege to the side of the opposition which was heretofore unprivileged. Now, the very stuff of politics is the maintenance of superiority or its destabilization. If deconstruction has the implication that all such oppositions are secret evidence of oppression, and if it carries the implicit exhortation to question each instance of such finally unfounded authority, then this will provide a further explanation as to why attempts have been made to locate Derrida's philosophical achievement with respect to the struggle against economic exploitation, sexual inequality and racial discrimination. Let us now examine each of these areas in turn, whilst asking at the same time how Foucault's theory of power fits into the picture.

Derrida, Foucault and Marxism

The Marxist argument against the separation of theory and practice is well known. As Marx put it, in the *Theses on Feuerbach*, the philosophers have only interpreted the world, but the point is to change it. Marx's thought developed in reaction to the classically Hegelian position that politics is inexorably borne along on the tide of history, a position that matches the helplessness of the historically determined political animal with the arrogance of the detached philosopher whose task is to explain the necessity of events after they have occurred. Even though unable to free himself entirely of Hegelian teleology, Marx's belief that people make history even if in circumstances not of their own choosing made possible a much closer relation between theory and practice, so that the 'truth' of a theory came to be seen not as a matter for post-factum theorizing, but as a practical question in the here and now. As he explained, it is in the only partially determined spheres of politics and ideology that struggles for this future rather than that one take place. The validity of ideas is determined in the material world by struggling to instantiate them in practices, not by enclosing them in hermetically sealed conceptual systems.

Marx's polemic against the skewed opposition between theory and practice can be seen as an instance of deconstruction:[2] the prestige of theory is challenged and made subject to the formerly derivative realm of practice. For Marx, no longer is the task to understand the transcendental logic of history through some theoretical schema that will present the truth of the world. The task now becomes one of realizing theory through practical struggle. It will not be enough to show *theoretically* how false the conception of, say, capital as a thing is, or even to go on and show its 'true' nature as a multiplex relation. For the theoretical demonstration will attain some level of truth only once it is enshrined in the practical-sensuous world.

To imagine that the validity and truth of ideas can somehow exist prior to their genuine material instantiation within existing society is to fall victim to the obfuscations of ideology. The 'Scientific Marxism' of the Second International (1889–1914) provides a prime example of this. Its proponents, especially Eduard Bernstein, felt that they possessed the scientific truth with regard to the relationship between the forces of production and the general nature of social and political life. Their theory told them that a further period of economic development was a necessary prerequisite for the transition to socialism. In its extreme form, the theory dictated that they could do nothing (except perhaps actively work to strengthen the capitalist economic system) to advance the arrival of socialism, and even Karl

Kautsky, a bitter opponent of Bernstein's 'revisionism', opposed Rosa Luxemburg's advocacy of the mass strike, writing (1983, p. 71): 'Today our agitation must escalate not towards the mass strike, but towards the coming Reichstag elections.' Marx himself may sometimes have been more flexible, arguing, for example, that science was a term which referred to 'knowledge of the social movement made by the people itself' (quoted in Jacoby, 1981, p. 21). But as the history of the Marxist movement shows, the power of conceptual hierarchies, like us and them, domination and resistance, science and ideology, is not neutralized by climbing from the low side to the high side. Becoming leaders rather than rabble, practising science instead of ideology, moving from violent revolution to a position of bureaucratic control, does not mean overturning the oppositions formerly suffered but now enjoyed. In fact, what can occur here is that the metaphysic may be taken as even more deeply confirmed, with the successful revolutionary party becoming even more certain than were the dominant forces of the old regime that truth and right lies with them and that 'the people' do not really know what is good for them. If the practical achievements of the Marxist movement are questionable, this perhaps is where the problem lies. In the so-called socialist societies the old oppositions have tended to remain just as unbalanced as they were before. The history of Marxism fails Marx's own test that the truth of its achievement be enshrined in the practical-sensuous world.

The advice which can be drawn from Derrida is to overturn the privilege of the high side and celebrate the secondary, derivative, low side: the supplement. As he (1981a, p. 93) tells us, 'Deconstruction is not neutral. It intervenes.' But Derrida's deconstruction does not provide a practical social theory which would indicate what such an intervention, such a celebration of the low side, might look like, or how it might be achieved. Additionally, the history of Marxism indicates that there are dangers in merely overturning a hierarchical opposition: there may be satisfaction and revenge in the aftermath of such an overturning, but is that enough?

There was a time when the concept of the dialectic had a certain attraction for Derrida (1981a, pp. 62–7). We are not talking here of that crude notion deployed by Engels in the schema of thesis-antithesis-synthesis – even if Derrida did once say that he was interested in certain crude forms of mechanical materialism (1981a, p. 50) – but rather of the very idea of

relationality. It was not long, however, before Derrida realized
that the dialectic tends to deny difference. It does this in its
aspiration to that moment of transcendence when the difference
between the two dialectically opposed moments is dissolved,
the ground of that dissolution being the yet-to-be-revealed
presence of each moment within the other. The horizon of
dialectics, then, is the resolution of difference.[3] In the case of
the Marxist dialectic, that resolution takes place in the liquid
movement of progress into the communist society. But the
lesson of deconstruction is that the resolution of difference
must only be the forced maintenance of a false appearance of
resolution. From the standpoint of deconstruction, a society
without difference could only be a closed society sustained
by force. Let us make no mistake, then, Derrida rejects the
communist ideal of a future society without power and without
difference.

Thus far, Derrida's thought would seem to be anti-Marxist;
and it is certainly the case that deconstruction provides the
critical concepts to undermine the mechanical historical determinism which lies at the root of much Marxist thinking. But it
is also the case that deconstruction opposes the diametrically
opposite view that nothing can be done about a repressive social
system. Derrida offers no reason to assume that a particular
system of differences – for example, the system of capital
and labour – is inevitable. Indeed, the very idea of historical
inevitability is anathema to the deconstructive programme.

This does not mean, however, that those critical Marxists
who celebrate subjectivity are necessarily right. We can follow
Michael Ryan, in *Marxism and Deconstruction*, and take Marcuse
as an example. His arguments anticipate a point beyond the 'per-
formance principle', beyond the subjugation of human faculties
to the profit-seeking logic of the capitalist system, where human
existence can be reoriented towards the achievement of entirely
different goals. For Marcuse, the principal aim will become the
attainment and maintenance of lives without constraint, and he
seeks to show the possibility of a non-repressive civilization by
examining the question of the libido and desire. He concludes
that the libido is inherently revolutionary and emancipatory, and
that this potential is blocked not by science and technology (i.e.
by the forces of production), which are potentially liberalizing
for the human spirit, but by the culture of domination which
we inhabit. This 'romantic anti-capitalism' (Kellner, 1984, pp.
372, 479) is based on the assumption that the human essence

is naturally both free and intersubjectively harmonious. If the repression is lifted then a life of joyous affirmation will be the automatic consequence. But this kind of subjective Marxism is rendered untenable by the thought of both Derrida and Foucault. For Derrida, the thesis of an original true essence is ideological, in the sense that it shares the very same assumptions which structure the metaphysics of presence in general. These assumptions are that a return to the true origin is both possible and desirable, and that those phenomena subsequent to the true origin are contingent and inessential. A political practice based upon the aim of returning to a point which will actually retreat to infinity must be, to say the least, questionable. Foucault's work on discipline adds to this critique, by showing to what extent the modern subject is implicated through and through in the capitalist project. It cannot be assumed that social beings are merely repressed by social structures, for they are essential and willing supports of these very structures.

The implication of this kind of thinking is that individual psychologies are not fixed. They may change. In just the same way as new social beings began to emerge at the beginning of the capitalist epoch, new social beings will emerge as and when our form of society begins to alter. The difficulty is that Foucault's perspective would appear to tell us that there is little prospect of bringing about such a fundamental change in a rational way; it is only in retrospect, he seems to say, that we can see how such changes have come about, and the deliberations of those who are seeking to make changes often seem to have been much less than central. How else are we to understand his view (1977a, p. 146) that the things which have value for us owe their existence to accidents, deviations, errors, false appraisals and faulty calculations? But, if this is the message of Foucault's work, would it not seem to be a recipe for political quietism? There lies a central problem, and probably the reason for the critique of the work of both Foucault and Derrida as conservative. We need not, however, be ruled by such understandings. At least the critique of notions of essential human nature, as authored by Foucault and Derrida, places us firmly in the realm of practice, telling us that this is where we are now, that we as social subjects are supports of the very structures that seem to repress. It can, of course, be said that we always knew this, or that Freud had worked this out a long time ago when he established that psychoanalysis was concerned with mental representations rather than with instincts. Precursors can always be found. Even if, however, we are not dealing with originality in its purest state, the lesson bears continual repetition; and there is more, for what Foucault and Derrida have done is to show how myths of origin and essence are a part of the basic social mechanism for the elimination of the threat (or promise) of difference.

The question is where do we go from here? Is there a positive practice that can emerge from such dark 'realism'? There is no easy answer to that question. The first thing to note is that the division of the world into artificial categories, like the economic, the political and the ideological (powerful symbols in the world of contemporary Marxism), or like the liberal division of government into the legislature, the executive and the judiciary, is an effect of power. These were categories that were fought over and struggled for. They may appear to be set in concrete, but this categorical certainty that we have in regard to the naturalness of ideas like the economy and the polity is underpinned by the metaphysical attitude that confirms the presence, analysability and manipulability of the world. It was perhaps the first glimmerings of a counter-understanding against this received metaphysic that lay behind the ultimately fruitless attempt by Soviet dialecticians to theorize a socialist science. Even though the results of this theorization may now appear quite ludicrous, with images of error-ridden post-capitalist genetics springing to mind, nevertheless the process did seek to apply a basic insight – the world is presented to us as what we think it is through the same process which makes us subjects within the structures, whether hierarchical or 'natural', of that world. So perhaps what matters most concerns the way we conceive things, and the minimal latitude that we might have for thinking differently. In his confrontation with Foucault, Derrida was saying that thought beyond the edge of thought was a hopeless ambition, but he was not saying that thought *on the edge* could not happen. He was encouraging precisely the opposite. If this remains a philosophical road, it is far from inconsequential.

Michel Foucault made an important point about Marxism. He said, in *The Order of Things*, that as a theory of knowledge and politics, Marxism is perfectly compatible with the general tenor of nineteenth-century thought (1970, p. 261). We can reveal this compatibility by considering some of the basic assumptions which are built into Marxism and which define its horizons. There is the assumption that political projects are capable of being finished; at its crudest, the building of a political party, for example, is taken to be analogous to the building of a bridge. Following this there is the assumption that when things go wrong, politically, it is always because the preconceptualization and planning was not careful or thorough enough. But what are the categories that are applied in the refinement of a political plan? Are they not categories like 'classes', 'the masses', 'the economy', 'the relations of production'? I place these notions in inverted commas because Derrida's critique shows that the promise that there is concrete reality behind them is actually a false promise. They are moves in a power play. Take a notion like 'the people'. When such a concept is used by a politician, it functions *as it always must* as a transcendental signified, a covert reference to a thing which is quite as unreachable as the angels; it cannot really point to the common needs and desires of a precise number of human beings without denying the differences among and between them. What operates then in political rhetoric, whether of the theoretical or of the demagogic or of the 'eminently reasonable' variety, is a kind of rhetorical dictatorship. General concepts are determinate orders, and fascism, liberalism and socialism have that in common (which is not to deny the very, very significant differences between them).

And what of the ideal of the communist society? Foucault's pessimistic theses on power reveal at least this: that the subordination of political practice to a future which is entirely unlike the present is fundamentally thoughtless. It is thoughtless in the way that someone failing to take any account of the diverse contingencies of the near future might nevertheless demand that everyone affected by this lack of thought acquiesce in the belief that things will turn out all right. An animal that did that would die, and if other animals followed in that course, they would die too. Foucault (1980, pp. 135–7) has made this general point in his discussion of Soviet labour camps, arguing that they cannot simply be wished away (and exposing in the process the rhetorical tricks that accomplish that particular piece of political deception), and asserting that they must be faced up to as a part of socialist reality.

It is possible that an utterly pervasive self-deceit, together with all but unrecognized rhetorical deception and conceptual violence, is functionally necessary for social life. Whether this is in fact so is one of the basic questions opened up by the Foucault–Derrida debate. Both Foucault and Derrida would accept that there is such blindness. Their reasons for that acceptance are different. Derrida sees that representation rests for much of its effect on the false promise that what is represented is ultimately redeemable. But this is a crime without a victim, there being no conceptualizable possibility of things being otherwise. Foucault holds that power relations are inescapable, and that concepts are no exception to that. Indeed he writes of the 'politics of truth'. Both can be described as radical thinkers, but neither has positive alternatives to offer against which the present system of knowledge or of society can be measured. Both are for and against Marxism: they are for Marxism because it exposes the false claims of the bourgeoisie to some kind of absolute truth and right; they are against Marxism because of the false nature of its main weapon which is the Utopian vision of a counter-society where all such falsehood will be eradicated.

Neither of them can be seen as traditional intellectuals. They have no place on which to stand in order to observe with any degree of detachment the society of which they are a part. Both, then, have been involved in the redefinition of the role of the intellectual in the age of suspicion against, what Lyotard has called, metanarratives. Both have formulated similar answers to the problem, and they amount to the view that the intellectual has to become more specific, more local. As Foucault (1977a, p. 208) has put it:

> theory does not express, translate, or serve to apply practice: it is practice. But it is local and regional ... not totalizing ... It is not to 'awaken consciousness' that we struggle ... but to sap power ... it is an activity conducted alongside those who struggle for power, and not their illumination from a safe distance.

Two strategies suggest themselves. First, in the knowledge that power is everywhere, and that one of its main operations is the construction of categories of people who are – so we are encouraged to think – naturally and rightfully repressed because such subordination is their lot, their fate, their just deserts (prisoners, homosexuals, the mentally ill, the unemployed, children, ethnic minorities, unbelievers, believers, women, the disabled, students, ecologists, conscientious objectors – this is no definitive list because there is no global theory that will hold these categories within the same general category, and the form of repression will vary from one to the next, and over time and place), the role of the specific intellectual will be to agitate for these many voices to be heard, using what residual status the intellectual has to facilitate that task. And it is not that each of these groups has just one voice. The process of labelling and stereotyping which underlies the categorization of such groups as the 'mentally ill', 'prisoners', and so on, is itself a politically momentous denial of the differences which exist between actually existing human beings. Somehow the specific intellectual has to lend weight to the disparate voices within groups at the same time as supporting the interests of the groups as a whole. This recognition of difference and identity at the same time cannot be accomplished by traditional forms of Marxist agitation, and furthermore it is discouraged by the metaphysical substructure of Western rationality (as Derrida has shown), and by the implication of subjects within that rationality (as Foucault has shown).

It may be thought that this first strategy is existentialist to a degree. John Rajchman (1985, pp. 36–8) has referred to it as an 'ethics of subjectivity'. It certainly seems to involve an act of will on the part of 'intellectuals' both to disencumber themselves from dominant social interests and to redefine their role as supporters rather than leaders. This might be seen as the personal–political corollary of deconstruction in so far as it involves the overturning of the personal priorities which are encouraged within hierarchical society.

The second strategy derives more from Foucault than from Derrida, and is more general than specific. It pertains to the question of the formation of social subjects, to the way that changes in social being have taken place over time, and in particular have taken place at nodal moments in the history of civilization. It is the equivalent of the warning at the end of the science fiction film, the warning to 'Watch the skies!' The point here is that we may, at any time, be on the brink of a major sociopsychological change. In the contemporary Western world, it may be that such a change is being dimly signalled by discussions of postmodernity, of information technology, of post-industrialism. If Foucault's lesson in *Discipline and Punish* is worth a thought, it is that changes in social formation are probably being accomplished *even now* by barely noticeable first steps in the formation of a new type of social being. There has been brief mention, above, of the positive side of hierarchical forms: they provide security, stability and predictability. If, however, hierarchies are becoming dysfunctional because of their inflexibility, their protection of non-contributory performers in key positions, and their discouragement of innovation – an absurdity within a mode of production where innovation is *the* motive power – they will be transformed. New modes of working will be found. But we know that non-hierarchical working is stressful: team-based social workers burn out, members of workers' co-operatives fall out, and the strains of working towards inadequately defined goals from within a structureless organization are presently intolerable. Functionally, one might even say from an evolutionist perspective, those changes in the socialization process (defined widely) which succeed in making individuals who can adapt better to formless working, controlled risk-taking, and not-infrequent disappointment (as the entrepreneurial ethos comes to define the many rather than the few) will be defended and dispersed by these first prototypes of what just might turn out to be a new form of social subject. Now, clearly this may be an overreaction to developments in the political, economic and educational practices of the Western world; and it is also obviously the case that such thoughts are massively ethnocentric. But, when placed alongside the recently emergent importance of the Master's Degree in Business Administration (MBA), about which Allan Bloom (1987, p. 370) has recently remarked: 'The effect of the MBA is to corral a horde of students who want to get into business school and to put the blinders on them, to legislate an officially approved undergraduate program for them at the outset ... Both the goal and the way of getting to it are fixed so that nothing can distract them', and alongside the increasing interanimation between education and economy (so that, in the UK, secondary education is extended by the provision of low-paid temporary training jobs in commerce and industry, with the probability of a concomitant growth of a new folklore which specifies this kind of behaviour rather than that as the secret of transforming a training scheme into a permanent job; and so that UK higher education students will become required to spend part of their undergraduate careers in the field of 'real employment'), the phenomena seem to be capable of at least an early hypothetical totalization. This second strategy, then, involves a watching brief on the modes of socialization; it involves continuously asking if they are changing, and how they are changing. It is Foucault who has taught us the potential significance of such changes: that what is at stake is the formation of new, better adjusted forms of social subject. This was always one of the weakest points within Marxism, that it hardly recognized the importance of processes of subject formation; it is to be hoped that a stress on processes of subject formation can form one of the strengths of post–Marxist radical thinking.

Feminism and Difference

The thought of Foucault and Derrida has had an impact on feminist thought, especially on French feminist theory.[4] Their theorizing has not been uncritically accepted. In fact, it has more often than not been rejected on those occasions when it has been considered directly. But their indirect influence has been considerable. The main reason for this pertains to their shared concern for recognizing and affirming difference. Derrida's advocacy of difference begins with his crusade against the dissolution of writing in the pure waters of speech. The philosophical subordination of writing by speech is important because it demonstrates the basic metaphysic which under-lies Western civilization. This metaphysic of presence does not tolerate difference unless it is accompanied by deference. Ultimately this metaphysic will deny value to anything other than self-effacing derivates of the Origin. It is not possible to specify all of the forms that the Origin takes, but among those that will be immediately recognized are God, nature and man. Deconstruction rejects the very notion of the Origin, as does Foucault. Both repudiate the ubiquitous practice of denying the specific being of what is different, opposing the general situation in which a full, present and powerful plenitude sustains its privileged position by parasitically sucking the life out of that upon which the myth of this power, presence and all-consuming adequacy is imposed. Speech denies any grounds for the autonomous qualities of writing; nature will be the measure of culture and will find it to be a lie; rationality will dismiss the claims of emotion, sympathy and intuition as pale, pathetic and unconstructive.[5] In each case a judgement is made by a self-appointed superior over a presumed inferior, and the judgement is always that the qualities of the inferior are in every respect inadequate and derivative copies of the superior instance. This is the story and process which deconstruction seeks to challenge, even if it does so only on the ground of theory.

It is a story and process which many women will recognize. From countless examples of women's writing, I choose the following statement from Mary Daly (1979, p. 29):

The fact is that we live in a profoundly anti-female society, a
misogynistic 'civilization' in which men collectively victimize
women, attacking us as personifications of their own paranoid
fears, as the Enemy. Within this society it is men who rape,
who sap women's energy, who deny women economic and
political power. To allow oneself to know and name these
facts is to commit anti-gynocidal acts. Acting in this way,
moving through the mazes of the anti-female society, requires
naming and overcoming the obstacles constructed by its
male agents and token female instruments. As a creative
crystallizing of the movement beyond the State of Patriarchal
Paralysis, this book is an act of Dis-possession; and hence, in
a sense beyond the limitations of the label *anti-male*, it is ...
Furiously and Finally Female.

It would be outrageous to suggest that Mary Daly's work has
been inspired by obscure debates within academic philosophy.
It has been inspired by an entire history of women in the
life-denying shadow of men, a history of women as insignificant
supplements to male presence, and a history of the modes of
violence through which the denial of reality to women has
been maintained. If Derrida's work recognizes that history,
this is no cause for congratulation. His work may perform the
marginally useful role of encouraging debate about difference
and about ways to overcome the oppressive (by definition) denial
of difference, but it may also be that the form and style of his
work function to negate its radical promise. We shall see.

It is fortunate that modern theory demands that we are spared
inquiring into the real intentions of the author. The death of the
author, as discussed by Foucault and others, however, does not
leave us just with the words on the page. We are also allowed
to speculate about the significant absences, about the words and
statements that are not put before us. We are able, as Althusser
reminded us, to treat a textual formulation as a symptom of its
underlying condition. Pursuing the metaphor, the surface marks
will only hint at the disease. They will not communicate all of
its deeper secrets. The pursuit of this approach is essential when
seeking out the political implications of the work of Foucault and
Derrida, and never more was this the case than in the particular
field of feminism. For if there are lessons for feminism (or any
other practical social movement, for that matter) in their work,
they do not reside on the surface. The work of Foucault will be
somewhat easier to treat than that of Derrida. At least Foucault

has interwoven the questions of sexuality and power. In both writers, we will find that the message for feminist theory lies in the pathos of their works (using that term in the sense that Derrida saw that the success of Foucault's quest to *know* madness lay in the pathos of his book, in its longing and in its failure).

Let me begin with the first volume of Foucault's *History of Sexuality*. It treats the nature of sexuality within nineteenth-century capitalism.

The advent of capitalism made sex into a productive force, controlled and confined within the utilitarian space of the parents' bedroom. Non-productive sex was abnormal, and to the extent that such abnormality could not be eradicated, it was subjected to the logic of profit and located in the sphere of brothels and pimps. Foucault asks if this is a repressive scene? Does it suggest the subjugating, life-denying power of the capitalist mode of production in ideological partnership with the clerical denunciation of pleasure for its own sake? Or is there something wrong with this view? Is it in some kind of underhand alliance with the very forces that it seeks to criticize? As soon as the focus is turned away from the repression of natural qualities towards the actual construction of the discourses of sexuality, Foucault found that rather than repression of discourses about sex, capitalist society witnessed a veritable explosion of sex talk. Underlying this explosion was the very creation of the form of sexuality itself.

The proliferation of sexual discourses can be seen in the state's increased concern for demographic detail, in the mounting consternation about childhood sexuality, in the architecture of schools and the planning of homes, in the development of gynaecology, psychiatry and the law, and in the emergence of coercive and potent models of normal and abnormal sexual behaviour.

From this merest sketch of Foucault's book, we can locate a number of critical absences. There appears to be little concern for pleasure in all of this, and there is certainly no conception of sexual pleasure as a right. This may seem to be quite in order, since after all his topic is the sexual attitudes of the Victorian era. In fact, the lack of any account of the ideology of sexual pleasure in relation to its possible function for the reproduction of patriarchal society points to a political lacuna. In Foucault's world, sex and pleasure go together even when they are riven apart within the austere confines of the Baptist household. Even here, there is an image of a certain sublimated pleasure in forbidding, watching for danger, and having certain knowledge of the evil of lust. In making the connection between power and pleasure, he does not develop this analysis into an account of patriarchy: his reason for avoiding this road is that his aim is not to reduce power to a single controlling function, but rather to pluralize power, finding it in every relation and at every level of the social formation. Nor does he attempt to outline a sexed conception of individual identity which goes beyond social stereotypes. Any difference between men and women is elided in his concern to show that the energizing of the sexual field has implications for the monosexual way that we come to define and understand ourselves. Foucault's implicit monosexuality remains undeconstructed, and the politics of sexual difference disappear behind the screen of a *general* sexual epistemology:

> The essential point is that sex was not only a matter of sensation and pleasure, of law and taboo, but also of truth and falsehood, that the truth of sex became something fundamental ... in short, that sex was constituted as a problem of truth. (1981, p. 56)

The unexplored patriarchalism depicted in Foucault's account links truth and sexuality by establishing an essential demand at the heart of the modern self. This demand is autosuggestive. It is the urge to confess, to tell of our imperfections. Foucault does not specify the model against which we measure our faults. But it is surely no coincidence that the symbol of the confessional is at its most powerful within the Catholic Church, an institution which epitomizes the patriarchal values of power, hierarchy, obedience, functionality and arrogant, God-given self-confidence.

Foucault is quite correct to speak of the importance of the confession for modern culture. As he says:

> The confession has spread its effects far and wide. It plays a part in justice, medicine, education, family relationships, in love relations, in the most ordinary affairs of everyday life, and in the most solemn rites; one confesses one's crimes, one's sins, one's thoughts and desires, one's illnesses and troubles; one goes about telling with the greatest precision whatever is most difficult to tell. (1981, p. 59)

Foucault's *History of Sexuality* is not a theorization of difference or an exploration of the limits of resistance within the bounds of Western reason. From a radical point of view, the most positive way to read it would be to take it as a further specification, beyond *Discipline and Punish*, of just how deeply the anti-difference mores of Western society are instilled within us. So that the book could be taken as stern education as to the size of the revolutionary task. As a companion to *Discipline and Punish*, however, it is more likely to be received as another helpless statement of the self-imprisonment of Western humanity.

It is possible to present a counter-view to this, and to argue that there are lessons to be drawn from Foucault's success in overcoming the view of power as repressive:

> There came into being a vast technology of the psyche, which became a characteristic feature of the nineteenth and twentieth centuries; it ... turned sex into the reality hidden behind rational consciousness. (Foucault, 1980, p. 185)

This conception of the production of sexuality by a multiplicity of discourses and forces undermines ideologies of sexual liberation. As Peter Dews (1987, p. 165) has put it, 'The very notion of such a liberation is part of our system of servitude.' But it is probable that feminism already knew this, without, however, extending the insight to the extent that all liberation movements would, by application of the Foucauldian model of power, be similarly compromised. On this reading of Foucault's first book on sexuality, global struggle for liberation is to be replaced by resistance without principle. Those last two words are important. If everything is product of power, then nothing is redeemable, and all one can hope for are brief periods of respite (and that may be to expect too much) from the overwhelming sameness of it all. There is absolutely no space for difference in this, no possibility of self-control. The road is open to pure despair or pure celebration, and which is taken might just as well be determined by the throw of the dice.

Nancy Fraser's judgement (1981, p. 286) is that 'Foucault vacillates between two equally inadequate stances. On the one hand, he adopts a concept of power which permits him no condemnation of any objectionable features of modernity. But at the same time, and on the other hand, his rhetoric betrays the conviction that modernity is utterly without redeeming features. Clearly what Foucault needs and needs desperately are normative criteria for distinguishing between acceptable and unacceptable forms of power.' Fraser's view seems absolutely correct. An indication of the dangers of resistance without principle is provided by some of Foucault's remarks in a public discussion, which took place in 1978, on the law relating to sexual relations with minors. In particular, his view (1988, p. 284) that, 'an age barrier laid down by law does not have much sense ... the child may be trusted to say whether or not he was subjected to violence', even allowing for the fact that it is presented here out of context, exhibits the kind of complacency that might be expected from someone who suspects everything and must therefore condemn nothing.

In the next volume of the *History of Sexuality* series, Foucault will find something in which to place a certain degree of trust. Having, as I have said once before, become the modern Descartes who will suspect everything, it will perhaps come as no surprise that the Cartesian manoeuvre is duplicated, and some resources for a bearable ethical life are found in the self. But this is to anticipate slightly, for what I now want to show is that Derrida for a time ploughed a similar furrow to the one cut in Foucault's first sexuality book.

Foucault was right to emphasize the importance of confession. The compulsion to tell what one is, to admit one's own shortcomings to others, to measure oneself against some tacit common standard, is a part of the metaphysics of identity that structures Western society. Derrida knows that. He knows that the art of confession is also an art of identity-affirmation, and an effective denial of difference as anything other than derivation and inadequacy. Even knowing that, he cannot help himself. His confession is written on a postcard.

In *The Post Card*, Derrida addresses in a personal way the question of his relationship to one woman.[6] He does this in the context and content of a series of postcards. As the writer, Derrida is well aware that he represents the active principle. His virility imposes upon a passive audience which can only receive. There is space here for a critique of deconstructive strategy, since speech can expect an active response while writing feeds on the disabling distance between addressor and addressee. But the opportunity is not taken. As if in mitigation of the power of writing, Derrida expressly (and how extensive the spread of postal metaphors is!) repudiates the temptation of concluding that his objective virility entitles him to say what the condition of woman is, and what solutions to that condition might be found. His essay is, as much as it could be (and the very fact that he is active, the writer, the sender, the deliverer, may well mean that his enterprise is doomed from the start) an attack on the 'normal' assumption that women are pathological in relation to the normality of the male.

Derrida also exposes himself: self-defined as a captive of the metaphysics which he criticizes but cannot escape, his vision of a particular postcard of Socrates *writing* while Plato watches, which is also a vision of male power as Plato's erection sticks in Socrates' back, and as the phallocratic tradition forcing itself upon Derrida himself, applies also to Derrida watching while his readers make their notes on his work. What Derrida exposes himself to is the undecidability of male power: is it his or is it over him, is it mine or over me? His position is indeterminate between renunciation and forceful assertion of male power. At least, however, unlike Foucault, Derrida acknowledges the existence of patriarchal power.

How do we make sense of what Derrida is doing, of his metaphysical deliberations, in the light of this undecidability? One way of seeing it would be to say that, even while knowing that wherever his philosophical explorations lead him he will remain in the thrall of Western metaphysics, he might nevertheless find a fold in its fabric, cutting through a double thickness into an outside that is not outside, but that might for a while seem that way. Such a place would not be an outside of reason, and therefore not a place finally immune to the depredations of power. It would be a place that the male/mail had not yet reached. The pain comes from realizing that a message sent from this pseudo-outside, a postcard from this new place, will cut a road right back to the heart of phallogocentric reason. Perhaps silence is the only answer. As Derrida said, early on in relation to madness, to speak is to betray. But, and here is a thought to play with, perhaps there are postcards which do not arrive at that place where of necessity they are all sent. Perhaps there is here a temporary respite from the appalling determinism of Foucault's vision (which interestingly presents us with an almost exact reversal of their respective positions in regard to the madness debate).

It is a fair question as to how one can base a political practice on such thoughts. The first answer that springs to mind is that one cannot. But when articulated with Foucault's view of power, and with his exhortation to local struggles, it does seem possible that one might consider considering what one might call the politics of the fold. By this phrase I mean to refer to that outside which may not escape, but which for the time being at least offers a certain distance from the centre as defined by rationalism and the Enlightenment tradition. Might this not be a way to think of the politics of feminism, as providing a temporary sanctuary and a certain distance from the Enlightenment's regime of truth?

But even so qualified a form of optimism is hard to come by when reading Derrida's work. For the other side of his view is that woman craves, in her way, for generality[7] just as much as the Enlightenment tradition craves truth. He writes:

> You are the mistress of the equivocal ... you wanted generality: which is what I call a child. (1987, p. 23)

This postcard message is to a woman. As soon as we read it are we not under its power, the power of the sender, of the male man? Is interpretation and use of this man's work to be seen as insemination? What kind of seduction is he talking about when he scribbles on his postcard, 'In the last analysis I do nothing that does not have some interest in seducing you, in setting you astray from yourself in order to set you on the way toward me, uniquely' (1987, p. 69)?

If reflexivity is the condition of deconstruction, still it would seem that self-knowledge cannot dissolve the contradiction of the power of the messenger. Derrida demands that we reject the seduction, block the emission and return the postcard unread. This cannot escape being the most subtle affirmation of power. Or can it? The request is clear: do not read me; my language inseminates; I have no choice. It is the condition of reason all over again. Is this duplicity, or is it just about as close to honesty as duplicity can get? If we believe him when he writes, 'I kill you. I annul you at my fingertips, wrapped around my finger ... it suffices only that I be legible' (1987, p. 33), are we to understand that this duplicity, this display of alternating aggression and care, is *the* social condition, the frightening social law that we all carry inside ourselves? Are we to believe, or in our darker moments even just hope, that all we can expect from the social world is the occasional period of remission from our terminal condition. If a feminist politics could be seen as a politics of the fold, would it not be a politics of remission? Are these even the right kind of questions to ask? Derrida does not know. He asks that we do not read him, or that we forget that we have done so (1987, p. 36). Is such a plea a testament to his striving for an honest duplicity, to his existential belief that there is an unbridgeable distance between each of us, the *angst* of which is only lifted occasionally during, if we are lucky, short periods of remission? Wouldn't these short periods of remission be just those times when pathos, of which Derrida spoke in regard to Foucault on madness, sustained a community blind to historicity?

He writes, 'It will end very badly, for a long time I have no longer been able to refind myself, and in fact I betray myself, me, all the time. All those idiots who do not know how to decipher, and who would willingly believe that I lead a very sheltered life ... but it's true, the disdain mounts from year to year and the disgust, and I defend myself against it in vain (disdain or disgust, no, something else because there is always mixed with it that kind of sad solidarity ... a despairing compassion ... don't even want to take a step outside' (1987, p. 42) Derrida admired the pathos of Foucault's book on madness, and thought that its success lay in that pathos, even while that pathos illustrated an impossible yearning for the outside of reason, which just happened to be the same yearning that duplicitously underlies the rationalist tradition. And yet he uselessly searches for the outside of where he is just as Foucault did in the madness book, places his trust in the woman–audience to see his despair. But gets no postcard in return, and that is finally just, for he, and we, cannot avoid desiring the death of the other at the same time that we desire to allow it in its specific difference. He is an example of tolerance and yearning at the same time as manifesting aggression and desire for the death of the other. He was hard on Foucault because he saw the dishonesty of opening up only the side that desires the life of the other; Foucault's work, for Derrida, dishonestly avoided the desire for the death of the other.

In the first volume of *History of Sexuality*, and in *The Post Card*, similar themes and implications emerge. We find a pessimistic essentialism in both texts. Both are ruled by a determinism of reason and history which offers no scope for anything other than unprincipled resistance in one case, and honest dishonesty in the other. Both these works offer only the hope of temporary respite from fruitless struggle. Their politics are those of hide-and-seek.

Let us return to Foucault's failure seriously to posit the difference between men and women, and to his hiding behind the quasi-objectivity of historical study in order to conceal, even from himself, his desire for the maintenance of the form of patriarchal sexuality. His relentless employment of the generic term 'man', and his refusal of any serious encounter with the idea of patriarchy, are just two indicators of that.

But perhaps this is too harsh a verdict. Just as he has asked not to be expected to remain the same, is there not also a sense in which Foucault deliberately used the quasi-objectivity of historiography to avoid dictating to others? Should his strategy rather be seen, not as an incitement to repeat, but as an encouragement to speak? If his work were seen in this way, then a constancy could be observed from start to finish, from madness through to Christian sexuality: *allow the other to speak for itself in the hope that it might speak difference*. Such a reading of Foucault's project would fit in with his normative thoughts on the contemporary role of the intellectual, would make intelligible his refusal (1980, p. 192) to attempt to spell out the significance of his work on sexuality for feminism, and might rescue a certain residual hope for a non-repressive world from the ruins of his debate with Derrida.

There is, indeed, in his last works, the suggestion of a certain Utopian residue. It pertains to the exercise of discipline, but this time it is not so much a question of an alienating imposition, rather one of normatively reinforced self-regulation. If the repressive hypothesis, and its underlying economic explanation in terms of capital's need for productive labour, were correct, one would think that the target for sexual control would be the adult male worker. However, this did not happen. The bourgeoisie first controlled themselves. They were subjected to the direction of conscience to a far greater degree than the workers. It was in the bourgeois family that the sexuality of children was problematized and that feminine sexuality was medicalized. The 'nervous woman' is a bourgeois figure, as is the child weakened through self-abuse. Thus Foucault will not accept that the deployment of sexuality was established as a restraint on the pleasures of others by the dominant class, they structured it around themselves in the first instance. There is the beginning of a lesson here, but in order to go further we must look to the second volume of the *History of Sexuality*, which presents a vision of sexual mores and the ethics of personal identity in ancient Greece.

One view of the difference between the sexual mores of puritan Christianity and those of antiquity is that the former approves monogamy and sex for procreation and disapproves of homosexuality, while the latter was not so rigid, even seeing sexuality as positive in contrast to the predominantly negative vision of Christianity. On this view, the praise of abstinence, virginity and lifelong chastity which appears in Christianity would not have figured in Greece and Rome. But this is not accurate. Foucault's perusal of Greek and Roman sources shows that sexuality was already associated (if not exclusively) with evil, and that the rule of procreative monogamy was quite common, as indeed was celebration of abstinence and disapprobation of same-sex relations. Key themes of the sexual ideology of Christianity were, then, in some way present in ancient thought. This does not, however, lead Foucault to say that there was no difference between us and them, nor that we merely developed what was already present. The situation appears to be that while the modern individual is the product of codes and forms of authority, the Greek was, in a deep sense, self-made:

> more important than the content of the law and its conditions of application was the attitude that caused one to respect them. The accent was placed on the relationship with the self that enabled a person to keep from being carried away by the appetites and pleasures, to maintain a mastery and superiority over them, to keep his senses in a state of tranquillity, to remain free from interior bondage to the passions, and to achieve a mode of being that could be defined by the full enjoyment of oneself, or the perfect supremacy of oneself over oneself. (Foucault, 1986, p. 31)

This conception of Greek self-mastery was applicable only to the free Greek man. Women were regarded as subordinate to free men in the natural order of city-state society. Because of this inferior ascription, the discourse of self-mastery, which recommended the proper form of ethical relationship to oneself, was addressed solely to men. It spoke only to men about their freedom and the proper exercise of their authority and their rights. Within this male ethics, a critical distinction was observed between active and passive. This phallocentric distinction placed the honourable and moderate man on the superior, active side, with women, boys and slaves recognized as properly passive. For the Greek man, the principle forms of corruption were excess and passivity. Excessive behaviour, or in other words weakness in the face of the temptations of authority, was a clear indication of a lack of self-mastery; while passivity was deemed foreign to man's natural freedom.

Foucault's account of the relation between men and women in classical Athens is certainly oversimplified. It is probable that the norms pertaining to the relation between husband and wife were in a state of flux. On the one hand, the husband was bound by norms and some laws, but these apparently did not include only taking his pleasure within the marriage. He was restricted by the status of the woman he might seduce, since she would be regarded as the property, as wife or daughter, of another man to whom certain obligations would be owed. This could lead to the situation where the rape of another's wife would be potentially excusable while the active seduction and persuasion to a reciprocal affair with the same woman would be a much more serious offence, since it would constitute a greater challenge to the authority of the husband. On the other hand, general opinion was coming to expect that male behaviour would change as marriage impended. Moralists wrote that married men were not entitled to take their pleasure outside marriage. Why this countervailing attitude? Perhaps the old division of labour was breaking down, with strict divisions between mistress, concubine and wife becoming less common, and with the wife increasingly idealized in the spheres of love *and* beauty *and* pleasure *and* the household.[8] Even as it becomes the case, however, that new reciprocal obligations come into being between husband and wife,b2.509 the sources of those obligations are different for each. The wife's obligation derives from the husband, while the husband's derives from himself as master of his free self. The woman's virtue arises out of submissiveness, the man's honour from his strength.

Although the great common laws were present, as also were the contemporary if sometimes contradictory social expectations, there was something else. It inhabited what Habermas would call the lifeworld. It was a practice, a know-how that guided action by taking care of its needs, understanding their time, and heeding the wider responsibilities of the actor. If indeed it was the case that the free male citizens of the Athenian phallocracy had a developed sense of timing which attended to the needs and status of others for whom they exercised an active authority rooted in control over the self, then this cultural complex has long since been destroyed. Power without the exercise of such concomitant responsibility seems to be the rule of modern society. Now, if we take from Foucault and

Derrida the view that the reality of power brings us face to face with a political ontology of darkness, lightened only by occasional periods of remission, then the difference, described in the second volume of *History of Sexuality*, is that for the Greeks the abeyance of darkness is found through the nurtured resources of the soul in authority.

It may be argued that the general complaint against the present pertains to the use of authority (by men, leaders, capitalists, soldiers, politicians – by all of us at some time, in some way) without the automatic moderation of nurtured self-discipline. But if the subtext of Foucault's late work is that the most illuminating version of the radical critique of modern Western society is that we are no longer Greek, it remains the case that Foucault has identified a mechanism without a principle. What will determine the content of this ideal self held in check by itself? Despite this difficulty, the idea of self-discipline is worth exploring a little further.

Foucault's account of power holds that power relations are inescapable. If that is the case, *even if the idealized Greek male exercising power with responsibility is a total figment of the theoretical imagination*, might it not be worthwhile to inquire into the putative social structures which make such an unlikely phenomenon marginally plausible? Unfortunately, Foucault does not make a reliable guide here, for he all but ignores the brute division between the elite and the mass. We must bear this in mind when examining the way in which such responsible attitudes might have been nurtured.

What is training for the permanent (and, from the perspective of the Western male, possibly exhausting and daunting) regime of self-mastery? There was nothing specific for the sexual self. Rather the total regimen was deemed to be a training regimen for the control of desires, for the running of the household and for the governance of the city. There appears to be a pyramid of development, with the 'care of the self' being the initial but most difficult phase to conclude satisfactorily:

Self-mastery and the mastery of others were regarded as having the same form; since one was expected to govern oneself in the same manner as one governed one's household and played one's role in the city, it followed that the development of personal virtues, of *enkrateia* [moderation] in particular, was not essentially different from the development that enabled one to rise above other citizens to a position of leadership. The same apprenticeship ought to make a man both capable of virtue and capable of exercising power. (Foucault, 1986, pp. 75-6)

Socialization into the attitude of moderation and self-discipline was through the imposition of a permanent self-examination, a continual battle against the self, a 'solo contest'.[10] The stake in this contest is freedom. A self ruled by the desires is unfree. Therefore moderation equals freedom. Thus the exercise of self-mastery is closely connected to the state of freedom.

There is an essential relation, even isomorphism, between the ethics of self-mastery and the ethics of government:

> the freedom of individuals, understood as the mastery they were capable of exercising over themselves, was indispensible to the entire state ... The individual's attitude toward himself, the way in which he ensured his own freedom with regard to himself, and the form of supremacy he maintained over himself were a contributing element to the well-being and good order of the city. (Foucault, 1986, p. 79)

There are no final victories in either realm. Just as peace may be seen as the continuation of war by other means, so will it be necessary for self-mastery to be continually asserted. This relationship was to change with the advent of an ethic of purification, expressed in its essence by the Catholic cycle of sin, confession and redemption. Greek virtue was not a state of integrity or natural harmony/goodness, but a relationship of vigilant domination over self. But Greek self-mastery was replaced by Christian purification. Purification is oriented to the ideal of absolute purity. Its guiding principle is the definitive achievement of grace. For the Greeks, however, any victory over the constant pressure of desire can only be temporary. Training cannot be neglected once a battle is won. The war within the self is never over.

It is possible that the roots of a coming divide between theory and practice can be seen here. The ideology of purification, of emptying the self once and for all of everything that might be seen to be reprehensible, sets an impossible standard of being. The Greek man must know the truth about himself, but the measure is not the condition of absolute perfection, rather it is the strength required to continue a life of moderation and self-discipline in the presence of the continuing power of immoderate desire:

> one could not practise moderation without a certain form of knowledge that was at least one of its essential conditions. One could not form oneself as an ethical subject in the use of pleasures without forming oneself at the same time as a subject of knowledge ... Moderation implied that the *logos* be placed in a position of supremacy in the human being and that it be able to subdue the desires and regulate behaviour. (Foucault, 1986, p. 86)

While knowledge of oneself was essential, it did not take the form of an 'epistemological condition enabling the individual to recognise himself in his singularity as a desiring subject and to purify himself of the desire that was thus brought to light' (Foucault, 1986, p. 89). A practical resolution with regard to the self was required, not some quasi-ethical agonizing over one's dark side. For the Greeks recognized that self-mastery, not the total absence of desire, was the prime precondition for leading a life of moderation and reason.

The sources of this strength were personal, familial and societal. The virtuous Greek man sought to lead a life which displayed the beauty of its self-domination, demonstrating his refusal to be subordinate to the tyranny of his desires. The training for such a life was prefigurative, in the sense that all aspects of personal life were a preparation for *and* a public demonstration of virtue. One's worthiness to have authority over others was a matter of the highest importance; the sense of it was rooted in effective and overt self-mastery. Achieving such a life was dependent upon a continual effort of self-fashioning. It was, to use Foucault's term, an aesthetics of existence.

Let me repeat, however, that all Foucault identifies here is a mechanism without a principle, a force without direction. The problem of such an absence is that self-domination could lead one to do 'what has to be done'. Perhaps it does take self-discipline to sacrifice a generation or to cut off the village children's arms after the injections given by 'enemy' Red Cross workers. Without a normative regime, we cannot determine the essential parameters of self-discipline, and, as Derrida has reminded us, Foucault has tended throughout to ignore that aspect of desire that seeks the death of the other. The classical answer to such questions will refer to wisdom: strength and self-discipline are not enough. The resources of the *logos* are needed to give shape and direction to this power which has its foundation in self-mastery.

Within Foucault's vision of ancient Greece, women were capable of this self-domination, but institutionally and philosophically they remained in the shadow of men and the virile model of virtue. They could not aspire to represent the perfect form on account of their natural and social passivity.[11]

The masculine structure of moderation means that immoderation is opposed to the active principle. The essential nature of immoderation is passivity. Philandering might seem (to us now) as active; but it is not. It betokens a passive surrender to one's desires, and a passive refusal of exercising authority over oneself. Thus Greek stigma was not related to the object of desire, but rather to the intensity of the force with which it may be pursued. While the Greek domination of man over woman is undeniable, it is articulated with normative expectations and political ideals of self-mastery. Within an unacceptably severe structure of inequality, the value of self-mastery founded a high elitism characterized by moderation and responsibility.

Even supposing that this is just a story, can we learn from it? It may be said that Victorian capitalists did present an aesthetics of existence and an ethics of self-mastery, and that they did so in the context of a whole national society. It may also be argued that the ideology of the invisible hand functioned to rationalize self-disciplined capitalist behaviour as of great benefit to the society. But it is now the case, in late capitalism, that the corporations more nearly approximate to the normative environment of the city–state than do the national societies. One version of corporate life presents an intertwined ethics and aesthetics under the sign of the company. Is there space, or justification, or any sanction at all within that arena for a feminist movement? But perhaps such questions are too global.

Taking a different line, if periods of remission are all that can be expected, perhaps the aesthetics of existence is an appropriate concept through which to think of mechanisms of extending such interludes of peace and sanity. One thing is crystal clear in this context, and that is that extending such remission requires self-mastery and a disciplined focus on the positive rather than the negative.[12] It is rather as if a new social contract were required, but with the Greek addition that no such contract can be deemed to have been made once and for all. Any such contract between men and women will require continual renewal, and continuing efforts of maintenance. This too requires new dimensions of taking responsibility for self and others as the basis for a different kind of *modus vivendi*.

The postmodern critique of metanarratives asserts that there is no standpoint outside the system from which to judge it. Perhaps this is why Foucault's condemnation of the sexual inequality within the ancient Greek world is hardly in evidence. The Greeks no doubt justified male dominance on the basis of natural qualities, but as we saw in the case of Derrida's critique of the use of the concept of nature in Rousseau, such a justification ends up as no more than an ideology. The ideology of natural inequality is now unacceptable, but has it not been transmuted into an ideology of hierarchical superiority?[13] So that the question of sexual inequality is not now to be approached by denying natural inequality, but rather by attacking unearned assumptions of superiority on the part of those in power – economic, political, cultural, even parental. If it is a fact of statistics that a greater proportion of those in various positions of power are male, in one way their sex has little to do with it. As cases like Indira Ghandi, Benazir Bhutto and Margaret Thatcher show, sex is no absolute barrier. The important thing is to expose and decry the exercise of power without that form of care for others that begins from mastery of the self. This is the point of attack for radical social reformers. And if the tactics do not seem sufficiently radical, if they smack too much of reformism, it should be realized, as Foucault has pointed out, that just because a movement is co-opted does not mean that it has failed. Co-optation changes the functioning of power, and provides the platform for the next development.[14]

If Foucault's late work has, however, a political implication for feminism, it is probably not a direct one. Rather it is an arguably over-subtle message for men, or rather for those times when the powerful (and this is *all* of us at some times) are heedless of the needs, qualities and human reality of those over whom they claim responsibility and with whom they live and work. This message is that such behaviour is ugly and unbecoming in an honourable person. The question is how such a doctrine can be re-instilled within all of us.

After all of this textual excavation, we seem little nearer to elucidating a real politics of difference on the basis of the work of Foucault and Derrida. Foucault may have just pointed to a mechanism: the nurturing of self-discipline as one of the foundations of a good society. Derrida seems to give us merely honest duplicity. While it would seem that Derridean duplicity just might be tamed by Foucauldian self-discipline, we still lack the final clarity which would be provided by a concrete ethical standpoint. Finally, however, the way towards this will be provided by Derrida's writings on race.

Race and Difference

As a philosopher whose self-appointed task is the exploration and affirmation of difference, Derrida has encountered a major difficulty in regard to his recent analyses of racial inequality. His resolution of that difficulty has been finally to affirm a foundational principle of identity. Just as Foucault's final work testifies to the transcendent principle of honour, so does Derrida finally affirm that the limit of difference is reached with the unspeakable practices of apartheid. Derrida will now admit that certain configurations of the Other are beyond humanity. His declaration of enmity against state racism, and his understanding of 'the final solution' as *the worst*, point to something both constant and powerful within the human condition: this, in the final analysis, is nothing other than a general moral law. Vestigial it may be, and its invocation extremely rare, but for both Foucault and Derrida, there came a time when their duty was clear. In Foucault's case, the recognition of this duty is evidenced in his nostalgia for that Greek coalescence between the honour of the self and the honour of the city; for Derrida, this duty is acknowledged through his decision to write of oppositions which are beyond deconstruction, and in particular to affirm rather than deconstruct the moral superiority of Black over White in South Africa. Let us look more closely at what he has to say.

In 1986, Derrida helped to edit a collection of essays in honour of Nelson Mandela. In his contribution to that collection, he admitted that Mandela was a man to be admired, indeed that Mandela forced such admiration. He asked where that force came from. His answer was that it came from the rationality of his acts and from his respect for the law. Derrida writes (1987a, p. 15):

He presents himself in his people, before the law. Before a law he rejects, beyond any doubt, but which he rejects in the name of a superior law, the very one he declares to admire and before which he agrees *to appear.*

Derrida's view, then, is that we admire Mandela because of his ferocious admiration for that law above all state edicts: that human beings are created equal. Mandela, as a lawyer, can see that this supreme principle is enshrined within the writing of the law, but not the doings of the state officials. Here then is Derrida's admission: equality is written into Western reason but perverted by Western deed. What Derrida is saying is that Western reason, *at this point*, stands in no need of deconstruction. It is perfectly clear. Apartheid is evil, but not evil of reason since South Africa's written law is a perversion of reason, a perversion of the Western tradition wherein the legitimation of state constitutions refers back to the popular will. There is no erudite deconstruction of Rousseau's *Social Contract* here. The Western tradition is taken as unequivocal. *And, from the standpoint of the moral law, so it should be.*

It is important to note that Derrida does not here totally abandon his concern for affirming difference. The situation is that, confronted with the vicious difference of apartheid, Derrida now recognizes its limits, and implicitly allows that difference is contingent, at some level, on some minimal set of universal conditions. Mandela is saying that to be Black is not to be essentially different; but that Black is forced to be different; and that Black would wish the freedom to be the same; and that freedom would be the opening of the road to non-coercive (in either direction) difference.

Derrida's recognition of this law beyond the law allows him immediately to see why Mandela would not ally himself with those white liberals who wanted to try to reform the system from within. At this point, neither the Foucauldian argument for reformism, nor Derrida's micropolitics of remission, could be acceptable in a situation where the will of a few is so wickedly imposed on the bodies of the many, and where the founding violence of state formation is prevented from becoming history through its relentless daily repetition.

The situation is ironic. Face to face with the unavoidable demands of the moral law, Derrida applauds Mandela's call to dream the dream of Western reason. He quotes (1987a, p. 24)

Mandela's depiction of the origin, an origin perverted by Western interests:

> There were no classes, no rich or poor, and no exploitation of man by man. All men were free and equal and this was the foundation of government. Recognition of this general principle found expression in the constitution of the council ... in such a society are contained *the seeds of a revolutionary democracy* in which none will be held in slavery or servitude, and in which poverty, want, and insecurity shall be no more.

Derrida's appreciation and his support for Mandela's call for a return to the original democratic condition were also presented in an earlier essay against racism. He was asked to write an introductory piece for an exhibition entitled *Art Against Apartheid*, which opened in Paris in November 1983. In that essay, he makes a number of points. First, the exhibition indicts all of Western history. He did not fully explain what he meant by this. But in the light of his essay on Nelson Mandela, his meaning is now clear. It is that Western civilization has been the site of a massive contradiction between its values and its politics, its philosophy and its action, its creed of equality before the law and its actuality of inequality before the fact.

Derrida thus shows apartheid to be related to European state politics, an extreme development certainly, but a development therefrom nevertheless. He accepts that forms of rejection of the other may arise as racisms in other cultures, but he is clear that only European racism has formed a state racism, has made of itself an official doctrine. At this point, Derrida was not yet ready to defend Western reason against Western political history. He took the view that this state discourse of racism connects to a 'certain representation of nature, life, history, religion and law' (Derrida, 1986, p. 333). He developed that thought only to the extent of pointing out that, like all racisms, apartheid tends to pass segregation off as natural and as the very law of the origin. Such a critique of apartheid as deriving from the origin continues the deconstructive critique and accuses Western reason. It is from that platform that he goes on to suggest the interanimation of reason and economics. For the economic stability of Pretoria has been a precondition of European stability, through its gold and strategic ores, its strategic position with regard to the route around the cape, and its role in providing the employment created by the export of technological infrastructure like nuclear power stations.

Anne McClintock and Rob Nixon saw something unsatisfactory about Derrida's 1983 declaration against apartheid. They did not, however, anticipate Derrida's defence of the law above the law. Rather they felt that Derrida had chosen the word over the reality, and that he had too small an appreciation of the development of the official ideology of South African state racism. They argued that Derrida blurred historical differences by conferring a spurious autonomy on the single term apartheid. They thought that he quarantined the term apartheid from the historical process. They went on to point out that the official discourse of the South African state has ceased using the term, showing that the official discourse has moved through a series of stages, from the severely racist stage of apartheid (between 1948 and 1958), through a phase where the catchphrases were *separate development* and *self-determination* (1958–66), towards the apparent dismantling of apartheid through the introduction of the concepts of democratic pluralism and federalism. McClintock and Nixon suggested that the task should be to expose the contradiction between the development of the official discourse and the deepening brutality which lies beneath it. The discursive movement as a whole was to be seen as the abandonment of the language of apartheid in favour of a language of national difference. While McClintock and Nixon allowed that apartheid is a European condition (and saw this not as merely based on similarities between apartheid and, say, the West German treatment of Turkish immigrants, but as going deeper, even to address the very question of the normality of national boundaries), their view was that Derrida had been politically naïve, and that he had missed an opportunity to expose the fact that the discursive process in this case is entirely disingenuous, *saying* one thing to the outside world but *doing* another to the majority of the people. Derrida, they said, failed to communicate that even though South Africa's discursive strategy failed to erase the term apartheid from Western consciousness, the strategic deployment of terms like *democratic federalism* has had the function of appeasing some political consciences in the USA, and at least partially enabled a certain complicity to emerge between Reagan and Botha. In short, McClintock and Nixon say that Derrida ignored discursive realities like the fact that the language of South African racism now enables Pretoria to present the problem of the homelands as a classic

Third World issue of underdevelopment, with the solution to the difficulties being the promotion of long-term programmes of orderly urbanization, in favour of a liberal condemnation of apartheid and an expression of hope that the free market logic of capitalism will eventually bring it to an end. Such political naïvety is seen as playing into Pretorian hands.

McClintock and Nixon contrast the liberal view that capitalism will eventually bring apartheid to an end, with the 'revisionist' view that capitalism and apartheid are bound closely together, each feeding the other (the functionality of separate development is located here; it makes economic sense to draw upon the homelands for labour without taking *any* responsibility for the provision of a social infrastructure there). Additionally, by pointing to the plurality of separate homelands, the South African government can claim that the white minority is not in fact a minority at all.

Derrida's aggressively defensive response is a brilliant illustration of the workings of the deconstructive imagination. It shows his suspicion of reason combined with his willingness to use its every resource to win an argument. In fact, he has a very good case to make that his interlocutors ignored the context of his words, and that they crudely mistook an appeal for a description. But we are not yet dealing with the Derrida of the Mandela essay, and so he goes on to show that, due to the arrogant belief in the oneness of truth which is inscribed in the heart of Western reason, McClintock and Nixon refuse to appreciate either that multiple strategies are necessary or that apartheid can be simultaneously both functional and dysfunctional for capital. Derrida was perfectly clear what their critique amounted to: they wanted to restrict him to books and the library, leaving real politics to the 'activists'. He thus concludes his response (1986a, pp. 368–9) by associating his critics with the very structure that they feel themselves implacably set against:

> In short you are for the division of labour and the disciplined respect of disciplines. Each must stick to his role and stay within the field of his competence, none may transgress the limits of his territory. Oh you wouldn't go so far as to wish that some form of *apartheid* remain ... you obviously don't like this word ... you would favour instead reserved domains, the separate development of each community in the zone assigned to it.
> Not me.

Those last two words were prophetic. For, as we have seen, the Mandela essay sees him accepting the authority of the moral law, and applauding those who rigorously submit themselves to it.

We must, of course, be wary of assuming that the absolutely right view of racial difference is that it is a forced difference imposed upon an essential identity. This is hardly an original thought. It is open to the charge of ethnocentrism, and clearly open to deconstructionist rebuttal (Radhakrishnan, 1987). But, in the final analysis, the critical force of such concepts as ethnocentrism and phallocentrism inheres much more in the rejection of the imposition than it does in the affirmation of otherness. This may well be the case for deconstruction in general. If this is so, then we can say that deconstruction is at the end of its theoretical trajectory. Although its practical trajectory is another matter, for there are countless arenas where such a lesson needs to be learnt.

There are a number of signs that deconstruction's theoretical odyssey is at an end, and that the wheel has turned full circle, that we are back where we began. Just as Foucault sought to explain how it came about that the imagery of madness was constructed as it was, so we can now see contemporary scholars, who have worked their way through the works of Foucault, Derrida and others, coming to a very rapid appreciation of the links between economic interest and the construction of the other. Abdul R. JanMohamed, for instance, knows that racial stereotyping had an original economic base, and that racial perceptions changed radically as the slave trade developed, when 'Africans were newly characterised as the epitome of evil and barbarity' (JanMohamed, 1986, p. 80). His taken-for-granted understanding that the colonialist cognitive framework can be analysed in the terms of a series of deconstructible oppositions such as 'white and black, good and evil, superiority and inferiority, civilisation and savagery, intelligence and emotion, rationality and sensuality, self and other, subject and object' is, at least in part, due to the intellectual work for which Derrida has been responsible over the last two decades.

The work of Derrida and Foucault has contributed, in no small part, to the influential rethinking of orientalism by Edward Said. Asking whether difference can ever be postulated without invoking hostility and aggression is not, as some have suggested, to transform answerable political questions into unanswerable philosophical ones.[15] Perhaps one should ask questions which are capable of being answered. One such question would be whether any society has ever managed to accommodate difference without denying it. It may once have been thought that anthropologists might work towards an answer to that question but Said, following Foucault and Derrida, has shown that the anthropologist's categories are part of the power/knowledge complex, and this complex has been shown, by Derrida in particular, to be inescapably implicated in hierarchization and exclusion. Even though we do not know exactly where to proceed from here, we do have some sense of where we are.

This brings us back to the importance of Derrida's text on Mandela and Foucault's final writings on Greek ethics. In the absence of these texts, perhaps there would be some justification in arguing that both thinkers have specialized in confronting unanswerable philosophical dilemmas, and that the outcome of their predeterminedly fruitless thinking has been a sort of post-existentialist despair. If this was indeed a phase for them both, it was a phase which both finally passed through and beyond to a reaffirmation, all the stronger for having been so thoroughly tested, of that law above the law.

Their readers often sensed that what was being said had significance for political life, but it was always hard to see exactly what that was. We can now understand what should always have been obvious, that the difficulty of a political reading of Derrida and Foucault inheres not so much in what is written but more in what is expected of it. As the history of socialism, feminism and anti-racism should make plain, there are no simple solutions to what are extremely complex social constructions. But a general principle does come out of their work. That principle is that social philosophy must continue to address the rights of the other. It must continue to expose those epistemological and political practices which exclude the other in a multitude of subtle and not so subtle ways.

It is this principle that has underpinned most of the work that has been discussed in this book. It is, since the subject cannot be avoided, the apparent possibility that such a principle could be founded on moral turpitude that explains some of the dismay over the discovery of Paul de Man's wartime writings.

Derrida met the outcry over the discovery that Paul de Man, standard-bearer for deconstruction in the United States and professor of Comparative Literature at Yale University, had published over 100 articles in a pro-Nazi newspaper published in occupied Belgium, with a long article entitled 'Like the sound of the sea deep within a shell: Paul de Man's war'. In that article, written and published in 1988, Derrida makes plain that what de Man wrote was unforgivable. It is probable that de Man did not know of Auschwitz, even at the time of writing the last of these pieces in 1942. But there is no doubt that he did know about the oppression of Jews in Belgium, that they were forced to sell their businesses, that they were herded into just four cities, that they were subject to curfew and beaten up on the streets. Knowing that makes de Man's reviews of the writings of pro-Nazi ideologues deeply immoral. It makes his disparaging references to the inferiority of Jewish literature utterly reprehensible. His reference to a 'solution' to the Jewish problem takes us beyond words. For Derrida, there can be no question of forgiving and forgetting this. But beyond this, there is more to be said.

Derrida's response to the revelations concerning de Man's wartime writings is extremely complex. It was a much harder test of his philosophy and humanity than was the case with his writings on apartheid. In writing of Mandela, there was only his deep distrust of Western reason to overcome. As we have seen he did overcome this distrust, emerging on the side of reason to affirm the moral law. In dealing with de Man, however, the claims of justice and friendship were placed on the scales in a way that could never have been the case with his treatment of South Africa. Additionally, there is the undoubted fact that condemnations of de Man's past function in a very elaborate and disturbing way. To begin with, there is the matter of hypocrisy, that outrage in the US has to be understood in the context of an elite university system that has been guilty of its own past deeds of anti-Semitism and cruel racism. It also has to be recognized that criticisms of deconstruction which are allowed by these revelations of de Man's past may function to attenuate the political function of deconstruction, which has always been to expose the repression of the other as a contingent operation within the same. The essence of Derrida's response is that de Man did something unacceptable *but then entirely broke with it, and spent the rest of his working and writing life constructing a testament against his past.* As always, summary judgements will reveal not an instinct for justice, but the workings of self-interest. What de Man did should not be allowed to slide out of mind, but neither should it provide the occasion for blanket condemnation. The full complexity of the issues precludes the distillation of the issues into a simple formula. Is that not how we would all wish to be treated? And does this not remind us of Kant's famous formulation (Paton, 1948, p. 67) of the categorical imperative: 'I ought never to act except in such a way that I can also will that my maxim should become a universal law.'

Notes and References

1 Irene Harvey's view (1986, p. 113) that 'From these three sets of oppositions we can quite simply derive all others which govern the history of Western thought' is most unDerridean in the directness of its formulation. It is also quite misleading, since the very least that Derrida learnt from Foucault was to be much more subtle and cautious at those times when the former's penchant to a kind of conceptual determinism became difficult to resist.

2 Derrida's view of Marx has altered over time. While he began by holding Marxism to be yet another example of the metaphysics of presence, he gradually came to believe that Marx was seeking to expose the mythical foundations of capitalist domination in a manner quite sympathetic to Derrida's own procedure. For both thinkers, the key strategy of metaphysics has always been to dissolve uncertainties, differences and the complexities of social relationships, into grand and timeless concepts like capital, value, truth, economic efficiency, and so on *ad infinitum*. See Ryan (1982, pp. 44–6).

3 This is not the case for the 'negative dialectics' of Theodore Adorno. Adorno, like Derrida, sought to produce a fundamental change in the metaphysical substructure of contemporary thought. As Susan Buck-Morss (1977, p. xiii) has written: 'Adorno not only wanted to demonstrate the untruth of bourgeois thinking; he wanted to show that precisely when the bourgeois project – the idealist project of establishing the identity of mind and material reality – failed, it expressed, unintentionally, social truth, thus proving the pre-eminence of reality over mind and the necessity of a critical, dialectical attitude of nonidentity toward it.'

Whilst Martin Jay (1984, p. 22; 1984a, p. 526) has noted the thematic parallels between Adorno's thinking and Michel Foucault's work on the disciplinary society, the parallels between Adorno, on the one hand, and Derrida and Foucault, on the other, remain largely unexplored, even though this is an area of some importance with respect to the political implications of non-identitarian thinking. Michael Ryan's useful but brief exploration of their relationship includes the view that Derrida's thought is probably deeper since it challenges bourgeois thought on its own ground, while Adorno remains at the level of the social analogue of metaphysics (i.e. culture). A careful reading of Adorno's *Against Epistemology* would probably establish the untenability of this view (one recent commentator has written of how *Against Epistemology* is 'Adorno's attempt to show how epistemology betrays experience' [Valone, 1988, p. 87]); and, in any event, Ryan's conclusion here (1982, pp. 76–80) does slightly edge towards the very privileging of theory over practice which his book sets out to challenge. Peter Dews provides another set of marginal comments upon the relation between post-structuralism and critical theory, but his analysis is vitiated by his hesitation between the position that post-structuralism is constituted as a determined attack upon the very idea of subjectivity, and the position that 'post-structuralist thought can be seen to be more closely tied to the philosophy of consciousness than is the thought of Adorno, since it lacks any sense of the *interdependence* of identity and non-identity' (1987, p. 230) While it is overly simplistic to regard Foucault and Derrida as mounting a totally uncompromising attack on the philosophy of subjectivity, it is no answer to that rather facile position to offer the alternative misreading that their work lacks a sense of the interrelation between identity and non-identity, since it is precisely their concern with that relation that has led to much of their work.

4   For an indication of the influence of Derrida's thought on feminist theory, see Spivak (1981) and Felman (1981). Mary Jacobus (1981, p. 11) writes: 'deconstruction ... is the kind of work that's clearly productive for feminist theory. The education of ourselves in the very powerful and dominating way of reading and of writing enables us to identify where women have been silenced yet again in various ways'. Andrea Nye's view (1988, p. 195), while still approving, is more acute: 'The starting point of feminist play with the text was not a theoretical interest in the nature of language, but the painful and interested recognition of women's oppression ... Deconstruction was only a preliminary to the main task of the woman writer/thinker – the forbidden expression of her femininity. This would require what Derrida's metalinguistics could not allow – a language in which a feminine presence can make itself known.'

The influence of Foucault is even more diffuse than that of Derrida. Sonja Ruehl (1985) has made use of his work to understand 'the lesbian identity'. While Judith Butler (1987) has sought to analyse the construction of gender with the aid of his work, although it may be significant that in order to do so she has to locate a repressed Utopianism in his work. The feminist reception of Foucault has been quite contradictory, and the overall tenor is well caught, although with negative conclusions, by Toril Moi (1985): 'What could be more seductive for feminists than a discourse which ... focuses on the complex interaction of power and sexuality ... Alluring as they may seem, however, the apparent parallels between Foucault's work and feminism ought not to deceive us ... If we capitulate to Foucault's analysis, we will find ourselves caught up in a sado-masochistic spiral of power and resistance ... in which it will be quite impossible convincingly to argue that women under patriarchy constitute an oppressed group, let alone develop a theory of their liberation.' Approaching the Foucault-feminism connection in a more positive spirit, Irene Diamond and Lee Quinby, in their editorial introduction to a set of warily appreciative essays entitled *Feminism and Foucault*, write: 'feminist analysis clearly illuminates the seeming ubiquitousness of masculinist power over women. Foucaultian analysis exposes the effects of normalizing power in the production of human subjects. Both are necessary for a fuller understanding of power and possible paths of resistance. Another mutually corrective tension resides in the space between feminism's tendency towards utopianism and essentialism (through claims for a higher truth derived from women's experience) and Foucault's scepticism about emancipatory politics and inclination towards relativism. We would suggest that within these tensions one finds the potential for an ethics of activism that is particularly appropriate for challenging the Faustian impulses of the contemporary era: one that fosters a mode of empowerment that is at the same time infused with an awareness of the limits to human agency' (1988, pp. xvi–xvii).

5   Spivak (1979, p. 201) has written:

> In the interest of the effectiveness of the women's movement, emphasis is often placed upon a reversal of the public-private hierarchy. This is because in ordinary sexist households, educational institutions or workplaces, the sustaining explanation still remains that the public sector is more important, at once more rational and mysterious, and generally, more masculine than the private. The feminist, reversing this hierarchy, must insist that sexuality and the emotions are, in fact, so much more important and threatening that a masculinist sexual politics is obliged, repressively, to sustain all public activity.

6   It is notable that Anglo-American commentary on *The Post Card* has scrupulously avoided discussing the exchanges presented therein between Derrida and a woman/wife/lover. The book is actually comprised of three major essays: 'Envois', 'To speculate – on "Freud"' and 'Le facteur de la vérité'. The last of these essays is a critical discussion of Lacan and his seminar on Poe's *The Purloined Letter*. The Freud essay is an extended discussion of Freud's speculative text *Beyond the Pleasure Principle*. But 'Envois' is just a pile of postcards; 'sendings' as one might literally translate the term. As just a pile of jottings, they are easy to dismiss; Lingis (1985, p. 156) speaks of 'The untalented Joycean preciousness of *Envois*'; Norris (1987, p. 187) accepts the metaphor of the postcard ('What Derrida is suggesting ... is that we read the great texts of Western tradition ... as so many messages that circulate without any absolute source or destination') but has nothing to say about what accepting such a metaphor means in regard to Derrida's role as mailman/male man. It is precisely because the jottings in 'Envois' are cards for the mailman from the male man, that they deserve the attention which will here be given to them.

7   For an analysis of Derrida's essay, 'Spurs', which centres on Nietzsche's view of woman, see my 'Alcibiades as hero: Derrida/Nietzsche?' The critical passage (1979, p. 31), which discusses

the relation between woman and truth/generality, reads as follows:

> On the one side woman would be seen as castrated. The dogmatic metaphysicians of the male order would put forward the truth and the phallus as their special attributes. On the other side, woman would be seen as castrating, wielding the heavy knives of truth.

Derrida's recommendation in this earlier work was for woman, for the feminist movement, somehow to escape from the destructive alternation of art and truth. He did not advise how this was to be done; for the predicament was just the same as his own in relation to Western reason. As Spivak (1983, p. 173) has noted, 'When Derrida suggests that Western discourse is caught within the metaphysical or phallogocentric limit, his point is precisely that man can problematise but not fully disown his status as subject.'

8 Foucault explains that in Xenophon's *Oeconomicus*, one of the most important accounts we have of the Greek family in the classical era, we see that the household (*oikos*) includes more than the house. It includes fields, possessions, social relations. The centre of it all is economics as the art of 'commanding'. It is within this context that Xenophon discusses the relation between husband and wife. She is crucial for the good management of the *oikos*. But she may be only 15 when married. So the older husband has to train and guide her. Thus 'the marital relationship ... took the form of a pedagogy and a government of behaviour' (Foucault, 1986, p. 155). Each will have, by virtue of their separate natures, aptitudes to perform different functions in the *oikos*: the woman inside, the man outside (in the fields or in the city). How is the wife to retain herself as an object of desire against younger rivals, how will she keep her place in the *oikos*? She will do this by performing her duties well and in the right way. This will give her exercise, bearing and privilege within the *oikos*.

   To this can be added that the wife is the one who will be with her husband as a free person, not as a slave; and pleasures that are given freely are worth more than those which are obtained by duress. But there are degrees of freedom, and there does seem to be a contradiction in this classical argument, for if the wife remains under the authority of the husband, how can she give free consent?

9 While Athenian marriage was tied to the husband's status, imperial marriage was rather more complex. Foucault explores this change in the third volume of *The History of Sexuality*. In the Roman context of the first two centuries after Christ, the marital bond comes to have a new significance for the understanding of self. Pliny, for example, writes of missing his wife: *his sorrow and desire* for his absent partner testify to the general development of a more positive personal commitment to marriage.

In many other coeval texts marriage is shown as having taken on the character 'of a singular relation having its own force, its own difficulties, obligations, benefits and pleasures ... It has become a mode of relation between two partners ... marked by affective reciprocity and reciprocal dependence ... a matter of defining the way in which the husband would be able to form himself as an ethical subject within the relation of conjugality' (Foucault, 1986a, p. 155).

10 This struggle with the self, which is unceasing, and which is essential to both personal and civic identity, is a basic aspect of what Foucault meant when he said that the Greek *logos* had no other.

It is worth noting, at this point, that while the notion of struggle with the self has been of great importance for the work of Gilles Deleuze (about whom Foucault once said that the current century would come to be seen as Deleuzian) and Félix Guattari, whose *Anti-Oedipus* and *Milles Plateaux* were undoubtedly influenced by the anti-establishment aspects of Foucault's work, their conception of this struggle has been largely one of freeing the self from the petrified connections forced on to the self by a repressing society. Contrary to the spirit of *Anti-Oedipus*, Foucault's late work commends a responsibility towards power, a socially oriented self-discipline in the face of its temptations rather than an escape into the multi-connected inconstancy of a life modelled on the free play of schizophrenic desire. One should add, however, that in Guattari's writings on psychoanalysis and politics, there is recognition of the political sense in addressing the self as just as much a site of repressive tendencies as the wider institutional structures: 'the struggle against what we may call "microscopic fascism" – the fascism implanted within desiring machines – cannot be carried on via delegates or representatives, by identifiable and unchanging blocs. The face of the enemy is changing all the time: it can be a friend, a colleague, a superior, even oneself. There is never a time when you can be sure you are not going to fall for a politics supporting bureaucracy or privilege, into a paranoiac view of the world, an unconscious collusion with the establishment, an internalisation of social repression' (Guattari, 1984, p. 62). Unlike Deleuze (whose work in the 1980s has moved away from the Paris '68 influenced 'nomad thought' of *Anti-Oedipus* and *Milles Plateaux* towards an articulation of philosophical reformulations and various forms of cultural production resulting in two fairly technical volumes on the cinema and a recent book on Liebniz and the Baroque), Guattari has continued to remain interested in the articulation of subjectivity and institutional practices.

11 For a psychoanalytic account of the roots of this passivity see Mitchell (1974).

12 Richard Wolin (1986, p. 81) has implied that to draw such conclusions from Foucault's work is to embrace a 'decisionism' which 'rides roughshod over the trammels of social respectability and convention'. It is, however, precisely social values that

determine the agon of self-mastery in Greece, and sociopolitical change that brings about an alteration in this cultivation of the self as it was experienced in the Roman Empire (see Daraki, 1986).

13 Perhaps here is the explanation for Foucault's lack of attention to the notion and reality of patriarchy. Might it not be the case that one of the values from within the patriarchal ideology – viz. the value of rationalized superiority – has transcended the specificities of patriarchy and brought it about that the analysis of patriarchy as patriarchy is now redundant. What may now be required is a radical analysis of hierarchy as the immanent principle of Western society; it is at this point that Foucault's work on the technologies of the self meets up with Derrida's deconstruction.

14 For a fuller discussion of Foucault's thoughts on the necessity of co-optation for any process of structural change, see Gandal (1986).

15 The argument to that effect by Mani and Frankenberg (1985) is a deceptive piece of rhetoric. They provide no concrete examples to back up their assertion; and the fact is that in such cases as Palestine and Northern Ireland the political non-solutions all amount to a resort to violence. While there may be no guarantees that the search for philosophical resolutions to the problem of the coexistence of difference will yield miraculous results, the abandonment of that search is tantamount to capitulation in the face of manifold forms of self-interest.

Conclusion: Difference and the Other

The double trajectory of Foucault and Derrida, at times divergent, at times parallel, can finally be seen as a case of mutual complementarity. Their story began with a fundamental dispute as to the nature of otherness. For Foucault, the idea of the other expressed the tantalizing promise of difference and a new realm of being to explore. Derrida saw that Western reason has always relied, mostly in an unstated way, on the promise of a world of pure being, and he knew that such a promise could never be honoured. He attacked Foucault's Utopian aspirations to know difference in its pre-rational purity. Foucault was not happy to accept the critique, and his disparaging reply characterized Derrida as reason's lackey. But Foucault's work, after their direct exchange, effectively accepted that the whole being of difference resided in some obscured relation to reason, to politics, economics and the here and now of historicity.

From this point on, Foucault's work becomes more politically acute. After an interlude of epistemological clarification, he begins to treat sociohistoric developments under the sign of this-worldly transformation from one form of subjectivity to another. The lesson that he drew from *Discipline and Punish*, however, was devoid of any political hope. On whatever social stage, the central actors misrecognize their own importance; historical development was seen as arising out of functional adaptation to altering circumstances, but with the particular twist that the logic of change could never be grasped until its time was past. The political lessons of such teaching are hardly radical. The advocacy of local resistance to the ubiquitous networks of power was precisely aimless, since no model of an alternative social configuration was presented at this time. Those who read Foucault in the mid 1970s were destined to find no answers, merely a blanket authorization for any and every activity of political opposition.

His last books, however, do begin to present a counter-vision to the experience of modern culture. Like some contemporary

Descartes, Foucault offers the possibility, especially in *The Use of Pleasure*, that there are political resources within the self that have remained untapped and forgotten for millennia.

The regulation of the self, as a political principle, is a much less Utopian idea than the motivating concepts of social movements like Marxism or feminism. It builds on the analysis of power as ineluctable, and is also ameliorative with regard to Derrida's insight as to the destructiveness of desire. It declares that there is no such thing as otherness, except as a political-economic product at a particular point in history. It offers the possibility of a conceptual foundation for a new form of politics. Nevertheless, it is incomplete.

A double supplement is required. First, if history is seen as a sequence of determinations of otherness, any formulation of self-regulation must have built into it the imperative to challenge the hierarchically set regimes of otherness at any given time. The elimination of the historical tendency to create the other cannot be simply dissolved, but the hierarchical demotion of particular others can be continually challenged. Such challenges constitute the political imperative of deconstruction. They are also acknowledged by Foucault, who, in the context of a commentary on Kant's text 'What is Enlightenment?', had this to say:

> But if the Kantian question was that of knowing what limits knowledge has to renounce transgressing, it seems to me that the critical question today has to be turned back into a positive one: in what is given to us as universal, necessary, obligatory, what place is occupied by whatever is singular, contingent, and the product of arbitrary constraints. The point, in brief, is to transform the critique conducted in the form of necessary limitation into a practical critique that takes the form of a possible transgression. (Rabinow, 1986, p. 45)

Second, the Greek principle of self-regulation is just a mechanism without a rule for its application. It is fashionable to say that no such rule can exist, and in absolute terms that may be right. Foucault, however, was finally certain that the lack of an absolutely privileged standpoint did not mean that there could be no fresh ways of analysing our own world, no new initiatives to change that world, no practical innovations. He said as much when, while emphasizing that he did not look to the Greeks for total solutions, or even for an alternative or examplary case, he wrote:

> Among the cultural inventions of mankind there is a treasury of devices, techniques, ideas, procedures, and so on, that cannot exactly be reactivated, but at least constitute, or help to constitute, a certain point of view which can be very useful as a tool for analysing what's going on now – and to change it. (Rabinow, 1986, pp. 349–50)

If the task is to find a practical rule to guide the application of *other*-directed insights towards transgressive practices of social change, we are implicitly enjoined, by both Foucault and Derrida, to look to the Kantian formulation of the categorical imperative. We have seen how this conclusion may be supported by the tenor of Derrida's writings against racism. It can also be established by considering Foucault's commitment to ethics as 'a manner of being' (Rabinow, 1986, p. 377), by his practical political activities in support of prison reform, mental health reform, university reform, gay liberation – all of which work can be seen as his refusal to stand by and do nothing while others were being excluded, marginalized and treated as inanimate variables in the political equations of expediency – and by his statement, given in an interview conducted in Berkeley in 1983, in the context of a question about Heidegger and Nazism, that

> there is a very tenuous 'analytic' link between a philosophical conception and the concrete political attitude of someone who is appealing to it; the 'best' theories do not constitute a very effective protection against disastrous political choices ... at every moment, step by step, one must confront what one is thinking and saying with what one is doing, with what one is ... in fact what interests me is much more morals than politics or, in any case, politics as an ethics. (Rabinow, 1986, pp. 374–5)

What Foucault had to say, in 1983, about Heidegger's neglect of his own self, was repeated, albeit in a different register, by Derrida some four years later. His critique – and the weakness of the word is appropriate since the discursive ornamentation of Derrida's text bespeaks a certain tiredness – of Heidegger can be redescribed as a warning against erecting a metaphysical principle as supreme arbiter over the practical lives of human beings. Habermas (1989, pp. 449–50), appearing side by side with Derrida, puts the case clearly:

> Heidegger dealt with the theme of humanism at a time when the images of the horror that the arriving Allies encountered in Auschwitz and elsewhere had made their way into the smallest German village. If his talk of an 'essential happening' had any meaning at all, the singular event of the attempted annhilation of the Jews would have drawn the philosopher's attention ... But Heidegger dwells, as always, in the Universal. His concern is to show that man is the 'neighbour of Being' – not the neighbour of man ... [He] explains why moral judgements in general must remain beneath the level of essential thinking proper ... [He] strikes right through 'ethics' and reaches, instead, the 'destined'.

Speaking of Heidegger's 'Rectorship address', Derrida (1989, p. 470) puts it as follows (note where he places the italics):

> If its program seems diabolical, it is because, *without there being anything fortuitous in this*, it capitalizes on the worst, that is, on both evils at once: the sanctioning of Nazism and the gesture that is still metaphysical.

It would be unjust to suggest that the work of Foucault and Derrida be seen as mere footnotes to the *Critique of Pure Reason*. But their efforts may properly be seen as constituting the strongest reminder, for the contemporary era, that the totalizing powers of pure reason are both mythical and terroristic *no matter who lays claim to them*. Kant saw the necessity of thinking different forms of reason, in particular of thinking in a practical-ethical way. Foucault and Derrida, from their respective standpoints, finally approach the same conclusion. That neither of them would be happy to put matters in just that way, and would frame any agreement or disagreement within a series of parenthetical labyrinths, should not obscure the fact that both have worked to free the cultural field from its subordination to each and every doctrine of revealed truth, and that neither of them ever thought that any ultimate success would negate the possibility of arriving at contingent, practical rules and strategies for dealing with human dilemmas.

The full confluence of the ideas of Foucault and Derrida may never be achieved. But the vision, which is barely taking shape, of an aesthetics of existence oriented to the careful (in the fullest sense of the word) destabilization of hierarchical determinations of otherness, at least provides the possibility of an exit from the anti-social snares of liberal individualism.

Perhaps the achievements of the Enlightenment should not be underestimated, but rather should be built upon. Medieval myth and superstition may have been overcome, but new forms have been forced into the symbolic space of otherness. The ultimate lesson of the Foucault–Derrida debate is that there is no pure other, that ontological difference is a chimera. This means that there is no bright promise on the other side of reason. It also means, if all is on our side, that there is no reason, *outside of our reach*, why we cannot generate our own bright hope for a different future.

Bibliography

Adorno, Theodore (1982), *Against Epistemology* (Oxford, Blackwell).

Aronowitz, Stanley (1981), *The Crisis in Historical Materialism* (New York, Praeger).

Barthes, Roland (1972), *Critical Essays* (Evanston, Ill. Northwestern University Press).

Baudrillard, Jean (1983), *In the Shadow of the Silent Majorities* (New York, Semiotext(e)).

Bennington, Geoff (1979), 'Cogito incognito', *Oxford Literary Review* vol. 4, no. 1.

Benveniste, Emile (1971), *Problems in General Linguistics* (Miami, Miami University Press).

Bernstein, Richard J. (ed.) (1985), *Habermas and Modernity* (Oxford, Polity Press).

Beyssade, Jean–Marie (1973), 'Mais quoi ce sont des fous', *Revue de Metaphysique et de Morale*, no. 3.

Blanchot, Maurice (1986), *Michel Foucault, tel que je l'imagine* (Paris, Fata Morgana).

Bloom, Allan (1987), *The Closing of the American Mind* (New York, Simon & Schuster).

Boyne, Roy (1979), 'Alcibiades as hero: Derrida/Nietzsche?', *Sub-stance*, no. 26.

Buck-Morss, Susan (1977), *The Origin of Negative Dialectics* (Brighton, Harvester Press).

Butler, Judith (1987), 'Variations on sex and gender' in Seyla Benhabib and Drucilla Cornell (eds), *Feminism as Critique* (Oxford, Polity Press).

Carroll, David (1982), 'Disruptive discourse and critical power', *Humanities in Society*, vol. 5, no. 3/4.

Caton, Hiram (1973), *The Origin of Subjectivity: an Essay on Descartes* (New Haven, Conn., Yale University Press).

Cervantes, Miguel de (1950), *Don Quixote* (Harmondsworth, Penguin).

Cousins, Mark and Hussain, Athar (1984), *Michel Foucault* (London, Macmillan).

Coveney, P. J. (ed.) (1977), *France in Crisis: 1620–1675* (London, Macmillan).

Curley, E. M. (1978), *Descartes Against the Sceptics* (Oxford, Blackwell).

Dallmayr, Fred R. (1984), *Polis and Praxis* (Cambridge, Mass., MIT Press).

Daly, Mary (1979), *Gyn-Ecology* (London, Women's Press).

D'Amico, Robert (1984), 'Text and context: Derrida and Foucault on Descartes', in John Fekete (ed.), *The Structural Allegory* (Manchester, Manchester University Press).

Daraki, Maria (1986), 'Foucault's voyage to Greece', *Telos*, no. 67.

Deleuze, Gilles (1986), *Foucault* (Paris, Minuit).

Deleuze, Gilles and Guattari, Félix (1983), *Anti-Oedipus* (Minneapolis, Minn., University of Minnesota Press).

de Man, Paul (1983), *Blindness and Insight*, 2nd edition (London, Methuen).

Derrida, Jacques (1976), *Of Grammatology* (Baltimore, Md, Johns Hopkins University Press).

Derrida, Jacques (1978), *Writing and Difference* (London, Routledge).

Derrida, Jacques (1981), *Dissemination* (London, Athlone Press).

Derrida, Jacques (1981a), *Positions* (Chicago, Chicago University Press).

Derrida, Jacques (1982), *Margins of Philosophy* (Brighton, Harvester Press).

Derrida, Jacques (1986), 'Racism's last word', in Henry Louis Gates Jr (ed.), *'Race', Writing and Difference* (Chicago, University of Chicago Press).

Derrida, Jacques (1986a), 'But, beyond ... (open letter to Anne McClintock and Rob Nixon)', in Henry Louis Gates Jr (ed.), *'Race', Writing and Difference* (Chicago, University of Chicago Press).

Derrida, Jacques (1987), *The Post Card* (Chicago, University of Chicago Press).

Derrida, Jacques (1987a), 'The laws of reflection: Nelson Mandela, in admiration' in Jacques Derrida and Mustapha Tilli (eds), *For Nelson Mandela* (New York, Seaver).

Derrida, Jacques (1988), 'Like the sound of the sea deep within a shell: Paul de Man's war', *Critical Inquiry*, vol. 14.

Derrida, Jacques (1989), 'Of spirit', *Critical Inquiry*, vol. 15.

de Sade, Marquis (1966), *The Complete Justine, Philosophy in the Bedroom, and Other Writings* (New York, Grove Press).

Descartes, René (1985), *The Philosophical Writings of Descartes*, Vols I and II, trans. John Cottingham, Robert Stoothoff and Dugald Murdoch (Cambridge, Cambridge University Press).

Descombes, Vincent (1980), *Modern French Philosophy* (Cambridge, Cambridge University Press).

Descombes, Vincent (1986), 'The ambiguity of the symbolic', *Theory, Culture and Society*, vol. 3, no. 3.

Dews, Peter (1987), *Logics of Disintegration* (London, Verso).

Diamond, Irene and Quinby, Lee (eds) (1988), *Feminism and Foucault* (Boston, Mass., Northeastern University Press).

Digby, Ann (1985), 'Moral treatment at the Retreat, 1796–1846' in W. F. Bynum *et al.* (eds), *The Anatomy of Madness*, Vol. II (London, Tavistock).

Dodds, E. R. (1968), *The Greeks and the Irrational* (Berkeley, Calif., University of California Press).

Felman, Shoshana (1975), 'Madness and philosophy; *or* literature's reason', *Yale French Studies*, no. 52.

Felman, Shoshana (1981), 'Rereading femininity', *Yale French Studies*, no. 62.

Flaherty, Peter (1986), '(Con)textual contest: Derrida and Foucault on madness and the Cartesian subject', *Philosophy of the Social Sciences*, vol. 16.

Foucault, Michel (1961), *Folie et déraison: Histoire de la folie à l'âge classique* (Paris, Plon).

Foucault, Michel (1964), 'La prose d'acteon', *Nouvelle Revue Francaise*, vol. 23.

Foucault, Michel (1967), *Madness and Civilisation* (London, Tavistock).

Foucault, Michel (1970), *The Order of Things* (London, Tavistock).

Foucault, Michel (1972), *The Archaeology of Knowledge* (London, Tavistock).

Foucault, Michel (1972a), *Histoire de la folie à l'âge classique*, 2nd edition (Paris, Gallimard).

Foucault, Michel (1977), *Discipline and Punish* (Harmondsworth, Penguin).

Foucault, Michel (1977a), *Language, Counter-Memory, Practice*, ed. Donald Bouchard (Oxford, Blackwell).

Foucault, Michel (1979), 'My body, this paper, this fire', *Oxford Literary Review*, vol. 4, no. 1.

Foucault, Michel (1979a), 'Governmentality', *Ideology and Consciousness*, no. 6.

Foucault, Michel (1980), *Power/Knowledge*, ed. Colin Gordon (Brighton, Harvester).

Foucault, Michel (1981), *The History of Sexuality*, Volume 1, *An Introduction* (Harmondsworth, Penguin).

Foucault, Michel (1986), *The Use of Pleasure* (Harmondsworth, Penguin).

Foucault, Michel (1986a), *The Care of the Self* (New York, Random House).

Foucault, Michel (1988), *Politics, Philosophy, Culture: Interviews and Other Writings 1977–1984*, ed. Lawrence D. Kritzman (London, Routledge).

Frankfurt, Harry (1970), *Demons, Dreamers and Madmen* (New York, Bobbs Merrill).

Fraser, Nancy (1981), 'Foucault on modern power: empirical insights and normative confusions', *Praxis International*, October.

Frow, John (1986), *Marxism and Literary History* (Oxford, Blackwell).

Gandal, Keith (1986), 'Michel Foucault: intellectual work and politics', *Telos*, no. 67.

Gibson, Walter S. (1973), *Hieronymus Bosch* (London, Thames & Hudson).

Grene, Marjorie (1985), *Descartes* (Brighton, Harvester).

Guattari, Félix (1984), *Molecular Revolution* (Harmondsworth, Penguin).

Habermas, Jurgen (1987), *The Philosophical Discourse of Modernity* (Oxford, Polity Press).

Habermas, Jurgen (1989), 'Work and Weltanschauung: the Heidegger controversy from a German perspective', *Critical Inquiry*, vol. 15.

Hartman, Geoffrey (1975), 'Monsieur Texte: on Jacques Derrida, his *Glas*', *Georgia Review*, vol. 29, no. 4.

Hartman, Geoffrey (1976), 'Monsieur Texte II: epiphany in Echoland', *Georgia Review*, vol. 30, no. 1.

Harvey, Irene (1986), *Derrida and the Economy of Différance* (Bloomington, Ind., Indiana University Press).

Henning, E. M. (1982), 'Archeology, deconstruction and intellectual history', in D. Lacapra, *et al.* (eds), *Modern European Intellectual History* (Ithaca, NY, Cornell University Press).

Hirst, Paul and Woolley, Penny (1982), *Social Relations and Human Attributes* (London, Tavistock).

Husserl, Edmund (1970), *Logical Investigations*, Vol. 1 (London, Routledge & Kegan Paul).

Jacobus, Mary (1981), 'Introduction', *Yale French Studies*, no. 62.

Jacoby, Russell (1981), *Dialectic of Defeat* (Cambridge, Cambridge University Press).

JanMohamed, Abdul R. (1986), 'The economy of manichean allegory: the function of racial difference in colonialist literature', in Henry Louis Gates Jr (ed.), *'Race', Writing and Difference* (Chicago, University of Chicago Press).

Jay, Martin (1984), *Adorno* (London, Fontana).

Jay, Martin (1984a), *Marxism and Totality* (Oxford, Polity Press).

Kautsky, Karl (1983), *Selected Political Writings*, ed. and trans. Patrick Goode (London, Macmillan).

Kellner, Douglas (1984), *Herbert Marcuse and the Crisis of Marxism* (London, Macmillan).

Lentricchia, Frank (1980), 'Derrida, history and intellectuals', *Salmagundi*, vols 50–1.

Léonard, Jacques (1980), 'L'historien et le philosophe', in M. Perrot, (ed.), *L'Impossible prison* (Paris, Seuil).

Levin, David Michael (1985), *The Body's Recollection of Being: Phenomenological Psychology and the Deconstruction of Nihilism* (London, Routledge).

Lingis, Alphonso (1985), 'The pleasures in post cards', in H. J. Silverman and D. Ihde (eds), *Hermeneutics and Deconstruction* (Albany, NY, State University of New York Press).

Loeb, Louis E. (1986), 'Is there radical dissimulation in Descartes' Meditations?' in Amelie Rorty (ed.), *Essays on Descartes' Meditations* (Berkeley, Calif., University of California Press).

Lyotard, Jean-François (1984), *The Postmodern Condition* (Manchester, Manchester University Press).

Madison, Gary Brent (1981), *The Phenomenology of Merleau-Ponty* (Athens, OH, Ohio University Press).

Mani, Lata and Frankenberg, Ruth (1985), 'The challenge of *Orientalism*', *Economy and Society*, vol. 14, no. 2.

Marx, Karl (1973), *The Eighteenth Brumaire of Louis Bonaparte*, in David Fernbach (ed.), *Karl Marx: Surveys From Exile* (Harmondsworth, Penguin [originally published in 1852]).

McClintock, Anne and Nixon, Rob (1986), 'No names apart: the separation of word and history in Derrida's "Le dernier mot du racisme" ', in Henry Louis Gates Jr (ed.), *'Race', Writing and Difference* (Chicago, University of Chicago Press).

Merquior, J. G. (1985), *Foucault* (London, Fontana).

Midelfort, H. C. Erik (1980), 'Madness and civilisation in early modern Europe', in Barbara Malament (ed.), *After the Reformation: Essays in Honor of J. H. Hexter* (Manchester, Manchester University Press).

Mitchell, Juliet (1974), *Psychoanalysis and Feminism* (Harmondsworth, Penguin).

Moi, Toril (1985), 'Power, sex and subjectivity: feminist reflections of Foucault', *Paragraph*, vol. 5.

Montaigne, Michel Eyquem de (1958), *Essays* (Harmondsworth, Penguin).

Neaman, Judith (1975), *Suggestions of the Devil* (New York, Doubleday).

Norris, Christopher (1987), *Derrida* (London, Fontana).

Nye, Andrea (1988), *Feminist Theory and the Philosophies of Man* (London, Croom Helm).

O'Brien, Patricia (1977), 'Crime and punishment as historical problem', *Journal of Social History*, vol. 11.

O'Neill, John (1986), 'The disciplinary society: from Weber to Foucault', *British Journal of Sociology*, vol. 37.

Pasquino, Pasquale (1986), 'Michel Foucault [1926–84]: the will to knowledge', *Economy and Society*, vol. 15, no. 1

Paton, H. J. (1948), *The Moral Law* (London, Hutchinson).

Peters, Tom (1988), *Thriving on Chaos* (London, Macmillan).

Pike, Ruth (1982), 'Penal servitude in early modern Spain: the galleys', *Journal of European Economic History*, vol. 11.

Plato (1941), *The Republic*, trans. F. M. Cornford (Oxford, Oxford University Press).

Plato (1960), *Gorgias* (Harmondsworth, Penguin).

Poster, Mark (1979), 'Foucault's true discourses', *Humanities in Society*, vol. 2, no. 2.

Rabinow, Paul (ed.) (1986), *The Foucault Reader* (Harmondsworth, Penguin).

Radhakrishnan, R. (1987), 'Ethnic identity and post-structuralist difference', *Cultural Critique*, no. 6.

Rajchman, John (1985), *Michel Foucault: The Freedom of Philosophy* (New York, Columbia University Press).

Rorty, Amelie (ed.) (1986), *Essays on Descartes' Meditations* (Berkeley, Calif., University of California Press).

Rosenthal, David M. (1986), 'Will and the theory of judgement', in Amelie Rorty (ed.), *Essays on Descartes' Meditations* (Berkeley, Calif., University of California Press).

Ruehl, Sonja (1985), 'Inverts and experts: Radclyffe Hall and the lesbian identity' in Judith Newton and Deborah Rosenfelt (eds), *Feminist Criticism and Social Change* (London, Methuen).

Ryan, Michael (1982), *Marxism and Deconstruction* (Baltimore, MD, Johns Hopkins University Press).

Said, Edward (1978), 'The problem of textuality: two exemplary positions', *Critical Inquiry*, vol. 4.
Sedgwick, Peter (1982), *PsychoPolitics* (London, Pluto Press).
Shakespeare, William (1972), *King Lear* (London, Methuen).
Sheridan, Alan (1980), *Michel Foucault: the Will to Truth* (London, Tavistock).
Spivak, Gayatri Chakravorti (1976), 'Translator's preface', to Jacques Derrida, *Of Grammatology* (Baltimore, Md, Johns Hopkins University Press).
Spivak, Gayatri Chakravorti (1979), 'Explanation and culture: marginalia', *Humanities in Society*, vol. 2, no. 3.
Spivak, Gayatri Chakravorti (1981), 'French feminism in an international frame', *Yale French Studies*, no. 62.
Spivak, Gayatri Chakravorti (1983), 'Displacement and the discourse of woman' in Mark Krupnick (ed.), *Displacement: Derrida and After* (Bloomington, Ind., Indiana University Press).
Sprinker, Michael (1980), 'Textual politics', *Boundary 2*, vol. 8, no. 1.
Staten, Henry (1984), *Wittgenstein and Derrida* (Lincoln, Nebr., University of Nebraska Press).
Steinart, Heinz (1984), 'The development of discipline: discourse analysis vs. social history', *Crime and Social Justice*, no. 20.

Valone, James J. (1988), 'Against epistemology: a constructive look at Adorno's deconstruction', *Human Studies*, vol. 11.

Weber, Max (1930), *The Protestant Ethic and the Spirit of Capitalism* (London, Allen & Unwin).
Williams, Bernard (1978), *Descartes: The Project of Pure Enquiry* (Harmondsworth, Penguin).
Wilson, Margaret D. (1986), 'Can I be the cause of my idea of the world? (Descartes on the infinite and indefinite)', in Amelie Rorty (ed), *Essays on Descartes' Meditations* (Berkeley, Calif., University of California Press).
Wittgenstein, Ludwig (1961), *Tractatus Logico-Philosophicus* (London, Routledge & Kegan Paul).
Wittgenstein, Ludwig (1972), *Philosophical Investigations* (Oxford, Blackwell).
Wolin, Richard (1986), 'Foucault's aesthetic decisionism', *Telos*, no. 67.
Wood, David (1979), 'An introduction to Derrida', *Radical Philosophy*, no. 21.
Wood, David (1985), 'Differance and the problem of strategy', in David Wood and Robert Bernasconi (eds), *Derrida and Differance* (Warwick, Parousia Press).

Index

Adorno, T. 160–1
Archeology 55, 58, 64–7, 73, 76, 89
Aronowitz, S. 89

Barthes, R. 15, 105
Baudrillard, J. 121
Bennington, G. 88
Benveniste, E. 106–7
Bernstein, E. 127
Bernstein, R. J. 121
Beyssade, J-M. 89
Blanchot, M. 116
Bloom, A. 134
Bosch, Hieronymus 16–20, 25, 26, 35
Brant, Sebastian 17
Breughel, Peter 17, 20
Buck-Morss, S. 160
Butler, J. 161

Carroll, D. 35, 122
Caton, H. 52
Cervantes 22, 23
Cousins, M. 34
Coveney, P. J. 34
Curley, E. M. 51

D'Amico, R. 76, 88
Dallmayr, F. R. 121, 171
Daly, M. 135, 136
Daraki, M. 165
De Man, P. 3, 99, 101, 120, 158–9
De Sade, Marquis 16, 24, 25, 26, 60, 87
Deconstruction 1, 74, 89, 90–108, 116,
    125–8, 133, 135, 142, 152, 157–9,
    161, 165, 167
Deleuze, G. 82, 121, 164
Derrida, J.
  'Cogito and the history of madness' 1,
    56–60, 62–3, 65, 67–8, 70–1, 87–8
  Of Grammatology 98–104
  Positions 127
  The Post Card 140–3
  'Plato's pharmacy' 95–7
  'The supplement of copula' 106–7
Descartes, R. 1, 3, 33, 36–52, 54, 55, 60,
    68–74, 76, 77, 89, 95, 140, 167

Descombes, V. 35, 88
Dews, P. 139, 161
Diamond, I. 161
Digby, A. 32
Dodds, E. R. 63, 64
Durkheim, E. 81, 118
Dürer 16, 21

Erasmus 16, 22, 26
Ethics 2–4, 11, 12, 41, 47, 61, 82, 133, 140,
    144–5, 148–9, 150, 152, 158, 162,
    164, 168–9

Felman, S. 34, 74, 87–8, 161
Feminism 1, 123, 135–9, 142, 144, 150–1,
    158, 161–3, 167
Flaherty, P. 75, 88
Foucault, M.
  Archeology of Knowledge 65, 79, 85, 88,
    108, 120
  The Care of the Self 163–4
  Discipline and Punish 15, 34, 79, 95,
    108–9, 111, 114–22, 125, 133, 139,
    166
  The History of Sexuality: Volume 1: An
    Introduction 137–40, 143
  The Order of Things 67, 79, 82, 130
  The Use of Pleasure 144–50, 163
  Madness and Civilisation 5–89 and passim
Frankenberg, R. 165
Frankfurt, H. 50
Fraser, N. 139–40
Frow, J. 75

Gandal, K. 165
Gibson, W. 18
Goya 16, 24–6, 35
Grene, M. 51
Guattari, F. 82, 164

Habermas, J. 89, 121, 146, 169
Hartman, G. 73
Harvey, I. 160
Hegelianism 64, 88, 126
Henning, E. M. 65, 89
Hirst, P. 35

Hussain, A. 34
Husserl, E. 92–8, 119–20

Jacobus, M. 161
Jacoby, R. 127
JanMohamed, A. R. 157
Jay, M. 160

Kant 2, 160, 167–9
Kautsky, K. 127
Kellner, D. 128

Lentricchia, F. 65, 88
Levi–Strauss, C. 104–5
Levin, D. M. 121
Lingis, A. 162
Loeb, L. E. 49
Lyotard, J–F. 89, 121, 132
Léonard, J. 120, 121

Madison, G. B. 120
Madness
  madness and art 15–26
  madness and knowledge 12, 24, 36–9,
    46, 48, 50, 56, 57, 73, 81, 96, 137
  madness and literature 22, 26, 87–8
  madness and medicine 6, 11, 14–15, 27,
    30, 55, 77
  madness and morality 18, 29, 31, 41, 47
  madness and otherness 9, 16, 19–21,
    43–5, 49, 53–4, 59, 68, 78, 82–5, 124,
    144
  madness and psychoanalysis 51
  madness and reason 65–7, 71–2, 76, 94,
    108, 120
  madness and Roman law 89
  madness and sexuality 80
  madness and social order 10, 13, 32
  madness and the will 23
  madness and transgression 28
Mani, L. 165
Marx, K. 9, 106
Marxism 82, 87, 121, 123, 125–35, 160,
  167
McClintock, A. 155
Merquior, J. G. 32, 34, 120–1
Midelfort, H. C. E. 6, 10, 35
Mitchell, J. 164
Moi, T. 161
Montaigne 43, 44, 45, 47

Neaman, J. 34, 89
Nietzsche 26, 63, 81, 84, 87, 91, 162
Nixon, R. 155
Norris, C. 162
Nye, A. 161

O'Brien, P. 120, 121
O'Neill, J. 175
Otherness 6, 9, 10, 15–20, 22–3, 25–6,
  31–4, 41–4, 48, 50, 53–4, 57, 62, 67,
  70–1, 74, 77–8, 81–5, 88–90, 101,
  117–19, 124–5, 135, 140, 143–4, 147,
  149, 151–2, 154, 157–9, 164, 166–8,
  170

Pasquino, P. 122
Peters, T. 175
Pike, R. 34
Plato 36, 62, 91, 95–7, 101, 104–5, 108,
  114, 119, 141
Politics of the fold 142
Poster, M. 87
Power
  functionalist theory of power 121
  God as the epitome of power 40–3, 49
  new forms of social power 108, 110,
    112–15, 119, 138
  power and exclusion 28, 115, 132, 136
  power and knowledge 12, 14, 29, 33,
    44, 114, 118, 158
  power and morality 2, 3, 43
  power and patriarchy 141–2, 151
  power and reason 29, 36, 38–9, 42,
    49, 60–2, 97, 127, 132, 135, 169
  power and resistance 132, 136, 139–41,
    161–2, 166
  power and sexuality 138
  power and the self 146, 148–51, 164
  power and the text 75–7, 140, 142
  sexuality and power 137, 141, 161
  the end of power 60, 128, 141

Quinby, L. 161

Rabinow, P. 167, 168
Radhakrishnan, R. 157
Rajchman, J. 133
Reason 2–3, 12, 16, 25–9, 31–4, 36, 39, 40,
  42–4, 47–9, 50, 53, 55–65, 67–72,
  75–9, 81, 83–91, 94, 96, 101–2, 104,
  106, 108, 120, 123–4, 139, 141–3,
  149, 153–4, 156, 159, 163, 166,
  169–70
Remission 142–3, 147, 150, 153
Rorty, A. 175
Rorty, R. 121
Rosenthal, D. 51
Rousseau, J–J. 26, 91, 97–104, 120–1, 151,
  153
Ruehl, S. 161
Ryan, M. 128, 160–1

Said, E. 75, 157–8
Saussure, F. de 105–7
Sedgwick, P. 32, 34
Shakespeare 22, 24, 26, 44
Sheridan, A. 34
Spivak, G. C. 125, 161–3
Sprinker, M. 74–5, 89
Staten, H. 119
Steinart, H. 120

Transgression 53, 79, 80–2, 84, 89, 167

Unreason 13, 20–1, 25–7, 42–7, 50–1, 54, 59, 63, 66, 70–1, 90
Valone, J. J. 160

Weber, M. 7, 118
Williams, B. 51
Wilson, M. D. 51
Wittgenstein 57, 91, 119
Wolin, R. 35, 164
Wood, D. 89, 93
Woolley, P. 35